The Complete Beginner's Guide to

WINDOWS 95

David Flynn

NET.WORKS

NET.WORKS

Net.Works, PO Box 200
Harrogate, N.Yorks
HG1 2YR England
Email: sales@net-works.co.uk
UK Fax: 01423-526035

Net.Works is an imprint of Take That Ltd.

Published in association withMaximedia Pty Ltd (A.C.N. 002 666 579) PO Box 529Kiama, NSW 2533, Australia.

ISBN: 1 873668 28 7

10 9 8 7 6 5 4 3 2 1

Trademarks:
Trademarked names are used throughout this book. Rather than place a trademark symbol in every occurance of a trademark name, the names are being used only in an editorial fashion for the benefit of the trademark owner, with no intention to infringe the trademark.

Printed and bound in The United Kingdom

Disclaimer:
The information in this book is distributed on an "as is" basis, without warranty. While very effort has been made to ensure that this book is free from errors or omissions, neither the author, the publisher, or their respective employees and agents, shall have any liability to any person or entity with respect to any liability, loss or damage caused or alleged to have been caused directly or indirectly by advice or instructions contained in this book or by the computer hardware or software products described herein. **Readers are urged to seek prior expert advice before making decisions, or refraining from making decisions, based on information or advice contained in this book.**

Contents

Special Reader Offer
Windows Shareware & Freeware

Here's your chance to acquire a great software library to evaluate on your own home computer. The programs listed below are Shareware, which means you can evaluate them in your own time — and only pay a registration fee to the author if and when you decide to use the program regularly. Have fun — and learn — with your computer!

DISK WIN-1

WinZip - The classic shareware program for compressing large files such as documents and images into small 'ZIP' files which can fit onto a single floppy disk or be sent across the Net.

WinGO - Click the WinGO icon in your Task bar's tray for the fastest way to get to your most-used directories.

SuperMenu - Make the Windows 95 Start Menu come to you, wherever you are, by clicking your right mouse button.

StickIt - These sticky yellow notes are ideal for quickly jotting onto a name, phone number or other info straight onto your PC screen.

FinePrint - Save paper and ink by squeezing your printed pages onto a single sheet.

DISK WIN-2

Microangelo - Create your own Windows icons or use any of the thousands which can be found on the Net. This is a great way to personalise your PC.

PowerToys - Some of the guys behind Windows 95 cooked up these handy-dandy tools for their own benefit but they've since become de riguer on all the best Windows machines!

TrayIcon - TrayIcon is the smart way to start programs. Why dive into the Start Menu to launch them when you can click an icon sitting in the Task bar's tray?

TrayExit - Time to close those Windows? Click the TrayExit icon and you're outta there in a flash!

TopDesk - Murphy's Law says that whenever you want to get to the desktop there'll be a dozen windows sitting in the way. Click TopDesk for an instant pop-up menu of your desktop icons, then tell Murphy where to go!

WinImage - Fit more files on your floppies, up to 1.7Mb, with WinImage. It can also make dozens of quick copies of a disk from a single 'image' on your hard drive.

WorldTimes - See the time anywhere in the world — great for international business or that long-distance romance!

TrayDay - Windows 95 tells you the time, but TrayDay gives you the day and date at a glance.

DISK WIN-3

Includes: **WordExpress** - Award Winning Windows wordprocessor. Truly impressive professional word processing in a fast, friendly package. Top of the line features include WYSIWYG editing, fonts, columns, pictures, tables, and more. Great for students, business, and small desktop publishing tasks, too. Voted Best New Product and Best Word Processing Application for 1995 by the Shareware Industry Awards Foundation.

Windows Typing Tutor - Complete tutorial enables anyone to learn to touch type quickly. Charts your accuracy and speed in a series of lessons. Helps you familiarise finger placement.

DISK WIN-4

Darebase - Windows Database manager, uses and/or creates Microsoft Access (*.MDB) files. Stand-alone, but does not require Access.

Continued on page 123 ⇨

INTRODUCTION

Welcome to Windows 95!

People get excited about the strangest things. A football team sacks its coach and the fans are all a-buzz. A whistle-stop tour by a restored steam engine is a major event in the calendar of railway enthusiasts. For computer buffs it's the debut of new software — none more so than Windows 95.

You may recall the extensive media coverage of August 24, 1995, when the Windows 95 software was released onto the worldwide market. TV and radio stations reported excitedly on it, as did the newspapers. Perhaps you, too, were waiting for Windows 95 — or maybe you were just a by-stander, bemused or amused at how a computer program could become a headline story in the evening news.

However it happened, and whatever role you played, Windows 95 arrived with a roar of thunder and a promise to make computing easier, more productive and — believe it or not — more fun!

What exactly is Windows 95?

Windows 95 is a special computer program called an operating sys-tem. The operating system (often abbreviated to OS) is what makes your personal computer work. Without an operating system your PC would be an extremely expensive and not at all attractive paperweight.

When you turn on your PC, it's the operating system which instructs pro-grams to appear on screen. When you press a key on the keyboard or click with the mouse, the operating system tells the PC what to do.

The operating system also lets you run application software — specific programs for tasks such as writing letters, balancing your books, playing games and connecting to the Internet.

What's so great about Windows 95?

Windows 95 is the best operating system for your PC. It allows you to run the latest and most powerful software, while remaining exceptionally easy and intuitive to use.

Things weren't always so. Several other versions of Windows came before Windows 95, and before them we didn't even have Windows — just an old-fashioned operating system called DOS (there's a potted history of how we got here from there in chapter one).

None of these could fully unleash the power of the modern PC in the same way Windows 95 can. This is why Windows 95 is so revolutionary and why it excited so many computer users.

So why this guide?

This guide isn't for the sort of people who get all frisky at the thought of a new operating system. They're already running Windows 95 and have been since day one.

This guide, if the title hasn't already given the game away, is for beginners.

If you've just bought a new PC, it will almost certainly be running Windows 95. You may need a helping hand to get started, and this guide will serve as your introduction to Windows 95.

If you've been running a PC under DOS or an earlier version of Windows and have decided to step up to Windows 95, this guide will be a steadying hand to the new and the different.

If your school, college or office requires you to use a Windows 95 computer, this guide will quickly show you the basics so you can get on with your work.

Even if you're already using Windows 95 but simply want to do *more* with it, this guide will teach you some neat tricks.

You can read *The Complete Beginner's Guide to Windows 95* on the train, during your coffee break or, best of all, while you sit in front of your PC.

By the end of each chapter you'll have learned useful skills. By the time you reach the last page you may not get shivers up and down your spine whenever you think of Windows 95, but you'll be using your computer with confidence, working a little bit smarter and having more fun along the way.

Enjoy the journey!

David Flynn

If you have any comments or queries you can email me at:
david@wordsmith.net.au

CHAPTER 1

A Brief History of Windows

O riginally, windows were discovered when one of our prehistoric ancestors moved into a cave with a hole in the wall and liked the view so much that he bashed another few holes for effect.

That's all I know about "small w" windows. When discussing the history of Windows with a capital "W", on the other hand, I am on somewhat more solid ground.

As many people will tell you, computing has changed dramatically in a short space of time. If you learn a little about where we've come from in terms of personal computers and operating system software, you will understand why everyone is switching to Windows 95.

Remember when . . .

Let's step briefly back to 1981. The Iron Lady was Prime Minister, Prince Charles married Lady Diana.

We were lining up outside the cinemas to see *Chariots of Fire* and *Raiders of The Lost Ark*, amazed that the first space shuttle was orbiting in the sky above and bemused by the noise and fashion that was punk music.

Somewhere amidst all that, IBM released a thing called a personal computer. It cost several months' wages and when you flicked the ON switch you were faced with a single stark line reading:

C:\>

You had to figure the rest out for yourself. The only way to do anything was to type instructions onto the keyboard using a set of cryptic commands.

This was the first version of an operating system known as MS-DOS. The DOS stood for "disk operating system" because it had to be loaded from a floppy disk. The MS stood for Microsoft, a company founded six years earlier by a university drop-out named Bill Gates who had some funny ideas about computers.

These ideas have since netted him an estimated personal fortune in excess of $24 billion, making Gates the richest man in the world.

Opening Windows

Things stayed quiet in the bleak and bleary world of DOS until Microsoft released Windows 3.0 in 1990.

Windows was a friendly graphical user interface (abbreviated to GUI and pronounced "gooey") in which programs were represented by little pictures called icons. The many options for each icon appeared as lists or menus which were activated using a mouse.

More importantly, you could run several programs at once, each contained in its own window on the computer screen — hence the name Windows.

Microsoft released the first version of Windows in 1985, but things didn't really start rolling until the introduction of Windows 3.0.

This was improved in 1991 and released as Windows 3.1, and the next year a smaller update named Windows 3.11 came on the market — together these programs are now referred to as "Windows 3.x". They are still used on over 100 million computers around the world.

However, for various reasons, Windows still wasn't perfect.

To a large extent what it really did was "window dressing", because you still had to load MS-DOS in order to use Windows. This meant that even the most modern PCs were tied down to software written over ten years ago — and in the rapidly changing world of computers this was like trying to win the Le Mans 24 hours in a Model-T Ford!

Windows 95 comes alive

Windows 95 brought the operating system into the nineties, by doing away entirely with MS-DOS and its inherent limitations.

One of the biggest gains (among many) is Plug-and-Play, through which Windows 95 automatically configures extra hardware such as printers and modems, saving you a lot of legwork!

Windows 95 is a 32-bit operating system, which means that all Windows 95 programs (and Windows itself) are written in a computer code which can shuffle data at twice the speed of the old 16-bit partnership of MS-DOS and Windows 3.x.

Because Windows 95 can do things faster, it can deftly juggle several operations at once. You can be printing a letter, copying files onto your hard drive and surfing the Internet all at the same time. This is called multitasking.

Windows 95 is now definitively the best-selling software in the world, and has become the foundation for a whole family of operating systems.

Large companies run thousands of PCs connected through an industrial-strength version called Windows NT.

At the other end of the spectrum is Windows CE, a featherweight version used on a new breed of pocket-sized electronic organisers.

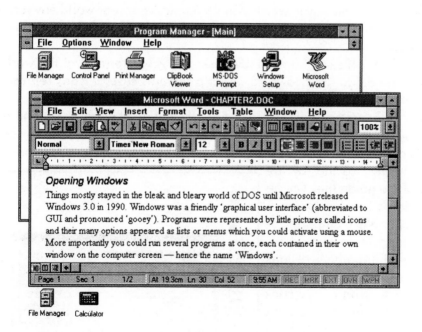

CHAPTER 2

A View Through New Windows

W indows 95 is the easiest way to use a personal computer. Much of this is due to the way in which Win 95 mimics your real-world environment.

For example, the main part of the Windows 95 interface is called the **desktop.**

Like your office or home-study desk, this is where most of the work gets done. The default Windows 95 desktop features several icons representing the various tools and resources at hand.

We'll discuss each of these icons briefly, but don't worry if you find things moving a little fast. In the following chapters the most important components of Windows 95 will be explained and explored using hands-on-tutorials and tips, so that by the end of the guide they will be completely familiar to you.

There's **My Computer**, or your computer to be precise.

Everything which resides on your PC's hard disk and any piece of hardware connected to the PC can be found by double-clicking on the My Computer icon to open it.

The PC's hard disk acts like a filing cabinet, storing

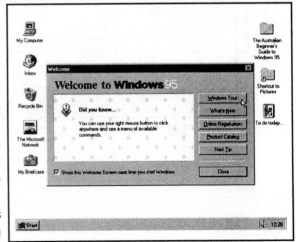

and organising your work in **files** and **folders** (called "directories" in Windows 3.x) which can have names up to 256 characters long. You can keep the files you refer to most often on your desktop, and when you've finished with a file simply dump it in the **Recycle Bin**.

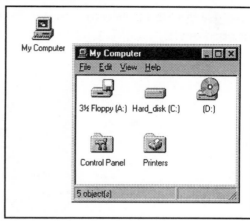

Windows 95 also comes with a **Briefcase** for moving files between computers (especially useful if you use a portable PC), and an **Inbox** designed to handle faxes and electronic mail.

The **Microsoft Network** is an online service which lets you venture onto the Internet (although there are plenty of other ways to get there).

The Windows 95 desktop can also be customised to include **shortcuts**, which provide instant access to any folder or document on your hard drive.

When you sit down at your office desk, you know how to begin the day's work. But what if it were your first day on the job? It would be handy if someone provided a box containing all the things you needed — all the bits of stationery, basic office equipment and instructions — to you get started.

That's where the **Start** button comes in. Click on this to see a pop-up menu which lists everything you can do in Windows — run programs, find or open documents, change the way your PC looks and works, and obtain help. (Oddly enough, you

BEHIND THE SCENES

Inside Windows 95 is a hidden salute to the people of Microsoft who developed this revolutionary piece of software.

Here's how to see it:

1. Right-click on the desktop, select New Folder and name the folder "and now, the moment you've all been waiting for" (not in quotes but otherwise exactly as written).

2. Right-click on the folder, select Rename and change the name to "we proudly present for your viewing pleasure".

3. Rename it again to read "The Microsoft Windows 95 Product Team!".

4. Now open the folder and watch the credits.

also use the Start button to stop Windows and shut down your PC at the end of each day!)

The Start button is part of a strip which runs all the way along the bottom of your screen. This strip is called the **Taskbar**, as it lets you switch between programs or tasks.

An elongated button appears on the Taskbar for every program you run. To switch between programs simply click on the appropriate button — it's just like changing channels on a TV!

At the far-right corner of the Taskbar is an area set aside for a handy group of small icons. This is the Tray, and the icons in it show the time, provide volume control for your PC's speakers, indicate the use of printers and modems, alert you to the arrival of Internet email and let you monitor or adjust the status of your PC in several other ways.

Where to from here?

★ First, read the *Introducing Windows 95* booklet, which should be included with your copy of Windows 95 or your new PC.

★ Next, click on the "Windows Tour" button on the *Welcome to Windows 95* screen which usually appears each time you start Windows. If there's no welcome screen you can click on the Start button, choose Help and select the option labelled "Tour: Ten minutes to using Windows 95" (you may need to have your Windows 95 CD-ROM at hand to see this guided tour).

★ Read this guide (yes, the one you're holding in your hands right now!). Set aside a little time each evening to read through these pages — ideally in front of your computer, so that you can follow the hands-on tutorials as you come across them. Read it through twice, if you can, to get the full benefit — and when you've finished put it on a handy bookshelf for quick reference.

★ Use the Help menu to learn more about Windows 95 as you go.

Stepping up from Windows 3.1?

Anyone with previous experience of Windows 3.x will discover that Windows 95 offers a very different way of doing things.

Where's the Program Manager?

Click on the Start button at the lower-left corner of the desktop. Up pops the Start menu — the "program manager" of Windows 95.

Software icons can sit on top of the Start menu or in groups sprouting from the Programs folder in the menu. This is where your Windows 3.x Program Manager groups will appear when you upgrade to Windows 95, and where the icons to start all new applications are found.

Unlike Program Manager groups, folders nested in the Programs menu can contain other folders — useful for keeping the main menu uncluttered.

Where's the File Manager?

Inside the Programs folder in the Start menu you'll find Windows Explorer — the primary tool for working with files and folders. Explorer offers easy file management, allowing you to view and work with the contents of your computer, as shown in the screenshot below.

You can learn how to use Explorer in our *Ten Minute Tutor* on page 31.

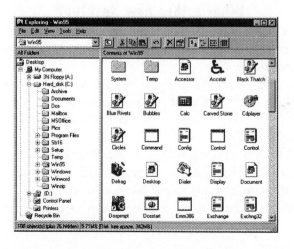

Where's the Control Panel?

Click on that ever-important Start button, select the Settings menu and open the Control Panel.

This bears close resemblance to its Windows 3.1 counterpart — with the addition of the Printers folder, which replaces the Windows 3.x Print Manager as the printing control centre.

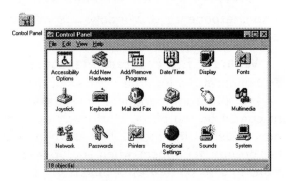

Where's MS-DOS?

Windows 95 is the first version of Windows to do away with the character-based MS-DOS operating system.

DOS is still there — look for the MS-DOS Prompt icon inside the Programs folder in the Start menu — but it's a stripped-down version which can launch Windows programs and recognise long file names. It even identifies itself as "Windows 95".

What's this new desktop?

In Windows 3.x the desktop was little more than a place to hang your decorative wallpaper. Windows 95 makes the desktop a vital part of the operating environment.

Files, folders and shortcuts to items on the hard disk can be stored on the desktop, which is in fact a physical location on your hard drive. (You will find it tucked away in a hidden directory called C:\WINDOWS\DESKTOP).

Also situated on the desktop is the icon for My Computer, which is where you'll find your disk drives (floppy, hard and CD-ROM) and your printer.

The Recycle Bin can also be found here, into which you can drop files to be deleted (with the option of recovering them at a later date).

What are shortcuts?

Shortcuts are icons which point to another object on your hard drive, such as programs, documents, folders and even devices such as printers. Simply clicking on a shortcut will run the object it points to.

Shortcut to Newsletters

Because shortcuts are small "detour" signs instead of the real item, they take up almost no space.

You can tell a shortcut by the curly arrow in the icon's lower-left corner. Shortcuts usually bear the title "Shortcut to ...", although you can rename a shortcut without affecting its operation.

Shortcuts can prove very handy — you'll learn how to create and use them in chapter 10, *Doing Windows Your Way.*

Why do I use the right mouse button?

In Windows 3.x you used only the left mouse button. You could select an object by clicking on it with the left mouse button, or drag-and-drop an object (you would do this typically when moving files in the File Manager) by selecting an icon, holding down the left mouse button, moving the mouse across the screen and at some point releasing the left button to drop the icon to a new location.

Windows 95 employs the right mouse button for clicking and "Drag-and-Drop", each time presenting you with a pop-up menu of options specific to the object you've clicked or dragged.

But don't worry, you can still use the left mouse button for dragging and dropping.

TEN MINUTE TUTOR

Start Here!

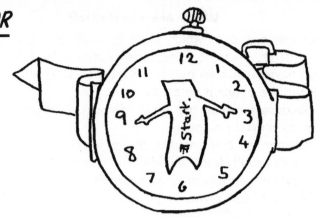

The Start menu and the Taskbar are the "dynamic duo" of Windows 95. Almost everything you do involves one or the other (or both) of these user-friendly controls.

Using the Start menu

One of the many difficulties in using any computer program is knowing where to start.

Microsoft solves this by whacking a great big button at the bottom-left corner of the screen with the word "Start" printed on it. Click on Start with your left mouse button to see the menu.

The Programs icon on the Start menu is the fast way to run your Windows programs.

Simply click on Start, then on Programs to see a cascading menu of the programs installed on your computer. By clicking once on the program of your choice, Windows will load it automatically. The Programs folder can also contain other folders to keep the menu tidy and organised.

Click on the Documents icon to see a list of the last fifteen documents you've worked on. These can be wordprocessor, database or graphics files. Just click on the document name and it will load up, ready for use.

The Settings option provides access to the Control Panel, Printers folder and Taskbar options.

Find is useful for locating files which have been "mislaid" on your PC. See the Power Tip "Finding Files" on page 30 for a lesson on how to put Find on the trail of those

QUICK TIP

Any item on the Start Menu which has a little arrow to the right-hand side indicates a 'cascading menu' containing other items. These automatically unfold whenever your mouse alights on that item.

lost letters to Grandma.

Help runs the Windows 95 online help system. Make this your first port of call when you need advice on how to perform a certain task or fix a niggling problem.

QUICK TIP

You can access the Start menu from your keyboard by pressing the Ctrl and Esc keys at the same time, or, if you have a Windows 95 keyboard, hit the key with the Windows logo on it.

When you need to enter a command to launch software which isn't listed on your Start menu, use Run.

Shut Down is fairly self-explanatory — use it to turn off your computer at the end of each day or when you need to reboot (restart) your computer.

As you become more adept at Windows 95, you'll want to customise the Start menu to suit your own habits — see chapter 10, *Doing Windows Your Way* for nifty ways to do this.

Using the Taskbar

The main function of the Taskbar is to let you deftly switch between the programs or Windows you have opened. The Taskbar helps you get used to the concept of "multitasking" — being able to have more than one program open or do more than one thing at a time.

Let's have a quick look at how the Taskbar works.

Double-click on the My Computer icon on your desktop: notice that this creates a matching button on the Taskbar which shows that the program is in use. Now double-click on the icon which represents your PC's hard disk (the icon is usually named C: or Hard Disk). This opens a folder displaying the contents of the disk, and another long button appears on the Taskbar.

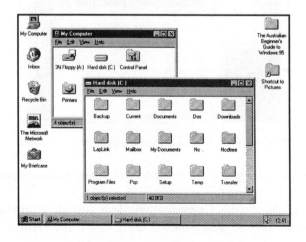

Click on the Start button and from the menu choose the Programs folder, then the Accessories folder, and finally click on the icon for WordPad. This opens a simple wordprocessing program supplied with Windows 95. Its Taskbar button is labelled "Document — WordPad".

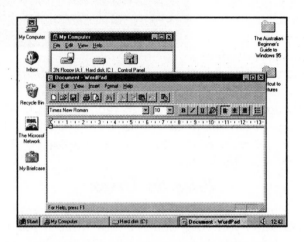

Dive back into the Accessories folder to run Paint and, in the Games folder, try Solitaire. Notice that for each new program you run, another button appears on the Taskbar.

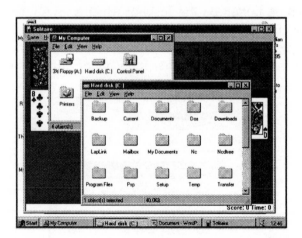

By now your screen looks cluttered as each successive window jostles for position in front of the rest.

To switch back to the My Computer window, just click on the My Computer button in the Taskbar and watch it jump out from behind.

Click on the Solitaire button to get back to your game of cards, or the WordPad button to hide the cards so the boss thinks you're hard at work.

QUICK TIP

Need to get to the desktop in a hurry? Shrink all open Windows into their Taskbar buttons by right-clicking on any vacant part of the Taskbar and choosing "Minimise All Windows".

The Taskbar buttons get smaller as you open more programs. If you need to increase the size of the Taskbar to accommodate more buttons, position your mouse cursor on the upper rim of the Taskbar until it turns into a double-headed arrow, then hold down the left mouse button and drag the Taskbar upwards.

What if you accidentally drag the Taskbar *down* instead of up and it disappears from view?

Look carefully at the bottom of your screen and you'll see a thin grey line — that's the Taskbar crouching down out of the way. If you move the mouse above this line this double-headed arrow will reappear. You can now drag the Taskbar back to its original size.

Using the Tray

The area at the extreme right of the Taskbar is called the Tray. It contains small icons which let you keep an eye on what's happening on your PC.

If you let the mouse hover across a Tray icon, information appears in a little yellow pop-up box.

Clicking, right-clicking and double-clicking on Tray icons leads to various actions and options, depending on the function the icon represents.

For example, the Speaker icon controls your PC's speaker volume — click on it once to change the volume or to temporarily mute the speaker, and twice to summon a mixer panel for volume and balance.

There's also a digital clock — let the mouse hover over the display and you'll see the day and date appear; double-click on it to access a calendar and clock where you can adjust the date and time.

Many applications add their own icons to the Tray, too. The screenshot below shows my (particularly busy) tray.

Some of these icons represent handy additions which I use every day.

Next to the speaker, for example, is an icon which shows that *Norton Anti Virus for Windows 95* guards against viruses.

The fuel gauge icon lets me keep an eye on how much of my machine's memory Windows has gobbled up at any one time.

The diary is another *Norton* program which schedules disk utilities to run at certain times.

I love the yellow note icon — it comes from 3M's *Post-It Software Notes*. One click and there's a digital version of those sticky yellow notes on the desktop.

Note that my tray displays the time in everyday format rather than the default military "2400" hour style. You'll learn how to change the format of your Tray clock in chapter 10, *Doing Windows Your Way*.

CHAPTER 3

Working With Files and Folders

The concept of files and folders is central to both the operation of Windows 95 and your PC.

A "file" is discrete chunk of computerised data — anything from a letter written on your wordprocessor to the wordprocessing program itself.

"Folders" (called "directories" in Windows 3.x) are where files are kept. In Windows 95 there are two ways to view the contents of a folder:

My Computer

Open My Computer and you'll see icons for your PC's hard drive, floppy disk and CD-ROM drive, as well as the Printers and Control Panel folders.

Double-clicking on the hard drive icon opens a window which shows the various files and folders on that drive. Note that the title bar of this window shows the icon and name of the drive.

Now, let's open a second window. Find and double-click on the folder named Windows in the hard-drive window. This calls up a window which overlaps the previous folder window and shows the various files and folders inside Windows. Note that the title bar of this window shows an open folder icon and the name of your Windows folder.

The default setting for each folder window is to display large icons with the file name underneath them — an approach which is long on looks but short on detail.

You can change this by selecting the folder's View menu and choosing to show the contents of the window as Small Icons, in List mode or in Details mode.

The View menu also includes an Arrange Icons option which orders these by name, type, size or date.

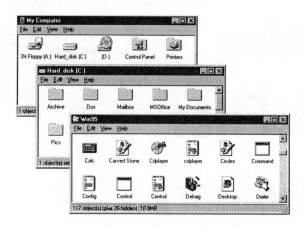

Alternatively, improve the view by choosing Toolbar from the View menu. This opens an iconic button bar (beneath the menu bar) which provides one-click access to display settings and file management features. Simply allow your mouse to hover over these buttons and a brief description of their functions will appear.

Go Exploring

Windows Explorer is the primary tool for handling files and folders in Windows 95. You'll find it in the Programs menu, accessed from the Start button.

Explorer looks similar to a folder window but includes a Tools menu and a "system tree" (in the left-hand window pane). Using Tools you can Find files or "Go to" (open) a certain folder; while the system tree allows you to inspect *everything* relating to your computer.

This makes the Explorer at once powerful and daunting — however, once you know a few tips and tricks you'll find Explorer easy and effective to use.

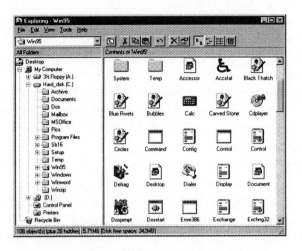

Our Ten Minute Tutor on page 31 will earn you an Explorer's Badge in no time.

Creating files and folders

It's easy to create a file or folder on your hard drive, on a floppy disk, or even on your desktop.

Position the cursor over an empty portion of a folder, desktop or the Explorer window — wherever you want the new file or folder to appear.

Click on the right mouse button and from the pop-up menu choose New, then select to create either a folder or a file of a particular type.

Naming files and folders

In Windows 95 files and folders can bear names up to 256 characters (including spaces) long. It's a welcome change from the days of Windows 3.x and MS-DOS, when you were limited to a name of eight characters followed by a three-letter extension (the "8.3" convention). This restricted you to file names such as DOCUMENT.TXT.

The new naming system is certainly handy, but there are some characters you can't use in a Windows 95 file name: the backslash (/); forward slash(\); colon (:); asterisk (*); question mark (?); double quotation mark (" or "); greater-than (>) or less-than (<) signs; or the vertical "pipe" symbol (|).

If you intend to run programs not designed for Windows 95 (or if you share your work with people who do so) be prepared to stick with the older naming convention, because Windows 3.1 and MS-DOS applications can only see a short version of the file or folder name.

For this reason a document called *January 1997 newsletter* will be saved in the Windows 95 filing system using two names — the long name and a truncated version which follows the 8.3 convention. This is created using the first six characters of the long name, followed by a tilde (~) and a number. The file extension is the default for documents created by the parent application. Therefore, a document called *January 1997 newsletter* created in a Windows 95 wordprocessor may show in a DOS program as *januar~1.doc*.

This is obviously going to lead to heartache if you have dozens of documents beginning with *January 1997*, because all any 16-bit application will see is a stack of files which are named *januar~1.doc*, *januar~2.doc* and so on.

What's worse is that when these files are opened and saved in an older program they lose the long file name altogether, so even your Windows 95 PC will see them as *januar~1.doc* or the like when they return.

Copying and moving files and folders

Do you need to shift a file or folder from one location to another? The easiest way to do this is to use the handy menu called up by the right mouse button.

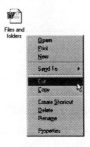

Select the file or folder, click on the right mouse button and choose Cut to remove the file, or Copy to duplicate it.

Now, position the cursor where you want the file or folder to appear, right-click and select Paste.

QUICK TIP

If you've opened a series of folders, one within another, you don't need to manually close each and every one. Simply hold down the Shift key while you click on the Close button on the last folder in the chain and they'll all disappear!

You can also use Drag-and-Drop. If you drag a file from one disk drive to another, such as from a floppy disk to a hard disk, the file will be copied (watch for the little "+" sign which appears next to the cursor). Holding down the Shift key, while you drag, forces Windows to move the file rather than copy it.

If you drag a file from one location to another on the same disk the file will be moved, unless you hold down the Ctrl key, which tells Windows to copy the file.

If all this gets a little confusing, just drag a file by holding down the right (rather than the left) mouse button as you move it — when you drop the file you'll see a pop-up menu from which you can choose Copy or Move, as befits the occasion.

Undo

If you accidentally copy or move a file, don't despair.

Simply pull down the Edit menu (or right-click on your desktop) and choose Undo to wind back the hands of time for your last few actions. This command also allows you to undo files or folders which have been accidentally deleted or renamed. Be sure to note that some Windows software only has one level of "undo".

Deleting and recovering files

There are two methods of deleting a file or folder.

Either drag it from a window and drop it into the Recycle Bin (which you'll find on the desktop) or select the object, right-click on it with the mouse and choose Delete from the pop-up menu.

Ooops — you've just deleted the wrong file? Don't panic. Double-click on the Recycle Bin to open the window showing its contents. You'll find the accidentally-deleted file here — select it, click on the right mouse button and choose Restore. Recycle Bin The file will be resurrected in its former location.

Getting around in folder Windows

The Toolbar is useful to:
   Display files as large icons;

Small icons; or

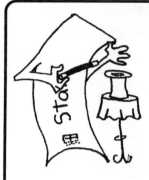

POWER TIP: RIGHT-CLICKING

Some of the most powerful features of Windows 95 are quite literally at your fingertips.

Instead of clicking on a file, folder or any other object with the left mouse button (common practice in Windows 3.x programs) try clicking once with the right.

Up pops a menu loaded with choices: Open; Print; Rename; Delete; Properties; and several others. Every object has its own menu with a unique set of options, depending on what Windows will let you do with that object. For example, if you open My Computer and right-click on the icon for your floppy drive, the choices include formatting and copying a disk. Right-click on the CD-ROM drive and you can even choose to eject a CD.

A detailed list, as shown in the screenshot below. This latter view allows you to sort files by clicking on a column heading. If you click on the Size column, for example, lists files from smallest to largest. Click the Size column again and the files now appear ranked from largest to smallest.

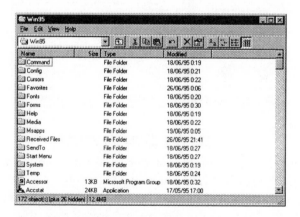

The toolbar (the line of icons under the program name) also allows you to arrange icons according to: name (in alphabetical order), type (such as Application, Bitmap Image and Text Document), the physical size of the file and the date it was created or last modified.

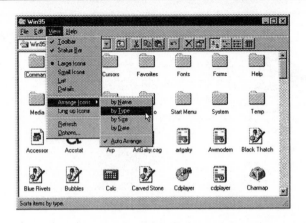

With the toolbar activated, look directly below the menus in each folder window. You'll see a drop-down list which displays the folders and disk drives on your PC. Click the small arrow at the right hand end of this list to quickly navigate your way around the system.

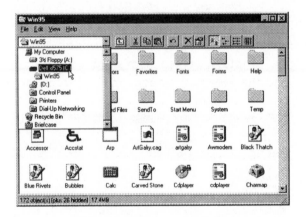

Using the Send To menu

The quickest way to move a file or folder from one location to another is by right-clicking on the object and choosing "Send To" on the pop-up menu. This cascades to reveal several locations which are pre-defined by Windows, including an option to send the file to your floppy disk drive.

This is a handy feature, right enough, but wouldn't it be more useful if you could specify your own "Send To" destinations? Here's how to do exactly that!

Use Explorer to open your Windows 95 folder, inside which you'll see a folder named SendTo. Inside this folder are shortcuts to each "target" which appears on the Send To menu.

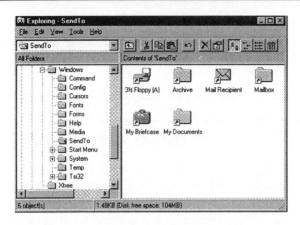

Do you want your My Documents folder to appear on the Send To menu? Simply create a shortcut to it inside the SendTo folder.

First, make sure you've clicked the Windows folder in Explorer so that all its sub-folders are visible — they have names like Command, Config, Cursors, Desktop and so on. The SendTo folder appears half-way down this list.

Move the vertical scroll bar (the bar which separates the list of folders and their contents) up, until you can see the My Documents folder in the left side of the Explorer screen.

Now, hold down the right button on your mouse and, as you do so, move the mouse down the list of folders — you'll see a shadow of the My Documents folder alongside the mouse pointer.

When the mouse pointer and "shadow" folder are sitting atop the SendTo folder (it will be highlighted) release the right mouse button. A pop-up menu will appear asking if you want to move the My Documents folder to this location, place a copy of it here, or create a shortcut here. Choose "Create Shortcut(s) here".

A folder named "Shortcut to My Documents" snaps into existence in the SendTo folder. Feel free to right-click the file, choose Rename and get rid of the "Shortcut to" preface. My Documents will now appear on the Send To list when you right-click on any file or folder.

Note that the exact meaning of "Send To" varies according to the location of the target and the file you've chosen to send. If the target and the selected file are on the same drive the file is moved — if they are on different drives the file is copied.

Moving files around your PC just became faster and easier!

POWER TIP: FINDING FILES

You know the feeling. You need a particular file — a letter, proposal or budget report — and you need it now. But what did you call it? Where did you store it? If your work is saved onto a voluminous network file server, images of needles and haystacks spring to mind.

It's times like these that the Windows 95 Find applet comes in handy. Select Find from the Start menu and choose Files or Folders (there's also an option to find information held on a specific computer which has been networked using Windows 95).

You can then specify any information you have available to narrow the search: the filename, possible location, date the file was created or last modified, file type or even a text string contained in the file. Once you've entered the

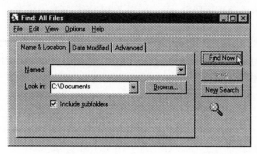

information, click on Find Now — and cross your fingers! It's even easier if you remember that Windows 95 lets you save the search pattern to re-use later.

TEN MINUTE TUTOR

Using Windows Explorer

With the help of Windows 95 Explorer you can browse through and manipulate everything which resides in, or is connected to, your PC — from hard drives and floppy disks to printers and networks.

There are several ways to run Windows Explorer.

You can open the Programs folder in the Start menu. You'll see the Explorer icon near the bottom of the program list.

A second way to open Explorer is by right-clicking on My Computer and choosing Explore from the pop-up menu. This trick also works with folders and disk drives.

Or, if you've already opened a folder and decide you need to be in "Explorer mode" for more detail, right-click on the menu icon (it looks like a tiny open folder and can be found directly above the File menu at the top left of the windows' title bar) and choose Explore.

Alternatively, if you have a Windows 95 keyboard, simply hold down 🪟 (the Windows logo) and hit E.

Once Explorer is up and running you can literally explore your PC by opening drives and folders in the left-hand window pane, and manipulating their contents in the right-hand pane (as in the screenshot below.)

Use Explorer's Toolbar to cut, copy, paste and delete files at a single click, to change the way files and folders are displayed, and to move up and down drives and special system folders.

If you view in Details mode you can change the order in which files are sorted by clicking on a column heading in the right-hand window pane.

Try it now: click on the top of the Name column to sort the files alphabetically from A to Z, and click on it again to sort them backwards from Z to A. This same trick lets you list files by size, type and date modified.

What do you do if you've done some exploring and still can't find a particular file? Simply click on the Tools menu for quick access to the Find utility.

Occasionally after moving or copying files in Windows 95 you may notice that the Explorer window hasn't marked these changes. Hitting F5 on your keyboard "refreshes" the display and brings the picture up to date.

The size of the open folder is marked in the status bar at the foot of the Explorer screen — but this is correct only if the folder doesn't contain sub-folders.

For example, when the Windows folder is selected, Explorer may report that it contains 150 objects and is 10Mb in size. These values don't take into account the desktop, nor the Fonts, Help, Media or System folders located inside C:\WINDOWS.

QUICK TIP

To select more than one file, hold down the left mouse button and "draw" a rectangle around the files (or folders) you wish to select.

You can find more accurate information by right-clicking on a folder in Explorer and choosing Properties. This will include all sub-folders and files in the tally.

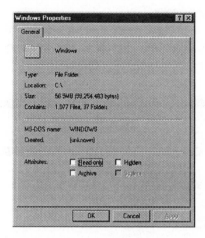

Moving or copying files and folders within Explorer is a cinch — if you know the tricks of the trade.

First, open the folder containing the file you wish to move, making sure you can see the file in the right-hand side of the window pane.

Next, scroll down the left-hand pane until the folder into which the file will be copied is visible — don't click on that folder, or you'll open its contents in the right-hand pane and lose sight of the file you want to shift!

Now, select the file in the right-hand window, then drag it across the window and drop it into the folder icon.

If you need to move a file to a sub-folder which isn't visible in the left-hand window, click on the "+" symbol next to its parent folder. This opens a list of sub-folders (providing you don't click on the folder itself) which you can then move the file to.

What if the folder you want to move to is too far down the list to be shown in the left-hand window pane when the file you want to copy is in the right-hand pane?

The solution is a nifty technique called "drag-push".

Select the file to be moved and drag it down towards the bottom of the left-hand pane — Explorer will automatically

QUICK TIP

To change the width of either Explorer pane place the mouse over the vertical divider bar and hold down the left button while you drag left or right.

scroll through the list to show you folders previously out of view.

If you're pining for Windows 3.1 File Manager, open your Windows folder and double-click on the file named WINFILE.EXE to see a familiar face.

But be warned: the Windows 95 version of File Manager will not recognise long folder or file names.

If you move a file or folder with a long name into File Manager it will adopt a truncated DOS name, which it will keep even when returned to Windows 95 programs.

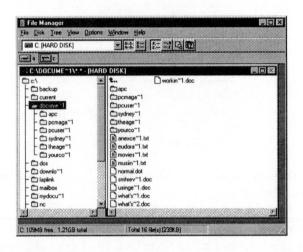

The best Explorer replacements by far are the commercial programs *Norton Navigator* and *MicroHelp PowerDesk's Explorer Plus*. Both combine the advantages of Windows 3.1 File Manager and Windows 95 Explorer.

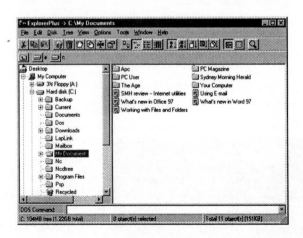

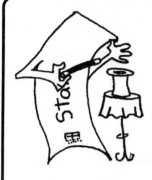

POWER TIP: EXPLORE ANYWHERE

By default Windows Explorer opens at your root directory — the "ground floor" of the C drive. This can be annoying if you consistently run Explorer in order to work with files in a particular folder, such as My Documents. To solve this problem, create a desktop shortcut which will open Explorer on a folder of your choice. Here's how:

1. Right-click on the desktop and choose New, followed by Shortcut on the cascade menu.

2. Enter the following command line:

Explorer.exe/e,C:\MyDocuments

(replace C:\My Documents with the name and location of the folder you want to work with). Click on Next.

3. Name the shortcut, and click on Finish. An icon will appear on your desktop.

4. Double-clicking on the icon will open Explorer with the focus on the file you've stipulated.

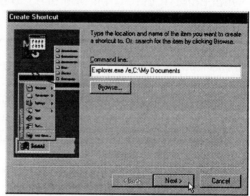

CHAPTER 4

Hardware for Windows 95

If you intend to buy a new PC to run Windows 95, exactly how much, and what kinds of, hardware will you need?

Or maybe you're planning to load Windows 95 on your current machine — what parts of the PC will you need to upgrade?

If you already have a PC

Microsoft states that the absolute minimum for Windows 95 is a 386DX with 4Mb of RAM.

Well, y-e-s — Windows 95 *does* run on such a system, but it's an experience which gives new meaning to the word "slow". It's almost impossible to use. Pull-down menus and dialog boxes take forever to appear, and the hard disk rattles away madly.

Only a 486DX/2, 486DX/4 or Pentium PC with at least 8Mb of RAM (or ideally 16Mb) has the necessary grunt for Windows 95.

You should have at least 500Mb of hard disk space — not just for Windows 95 but for all those new applications that you'll want to use with it.

Another area to investigate is your PC's video sub-system — the components which make the pretty pictures.

Graphics cards should have at least 1Mb of video RAM — but don't rush out to upgrade straight away as the new 32-bit drivers installed by Windows 95 often produce a remarkable improvement in video throughput. Wait until you've actually started running Windows 95 until you make this decision.

You may want to contact your PC manufacturer or consult its Web page on the Internet to find out if it has released an update for your PC's BIOS (Basic Input Output System) chip which will support Windows 95's advanced capabilities, such as Plug-and-Play. Check chapter 7 for instructions on how to connect to the Internet.

Where you may find the need to spend anew is on your monitor. The standard 14-inch screen really doesn't do justice to the Windows 95 desktop. A 15-inch monitor will increase your screen real estate by a whopping 36 percent, bringing Windows 95 to life!

If you're buying a new PC

Now that Windows 95 is almost 18- months old, PC technology has caught up to the operating system's heavy overhead.

It's impossible to buy anything new that's slower than a Pentium — the only choice is how fast the machine is. This is measured in the "speed" of the chip, rated in megahertz (MHz, or millions of cycles per second).

At the time of writing the common choices are 133MHz, 150MHz and 166MHz: the higher the number, the faster the PC. I recommend you opt for a 150MHz or 166MHz machine.

The march of technology has also seen memory prices plummet to the point where 16Mb of RAM is taken for granted. Almost nobody makes hard disks smaller than 1.2Gb, or CD-ROM drives slower than eight-speed.

Best of all, a PC with this muscle-bound specification costs about the same as much less powerful configurations did when Windows 95 was let off the leash. PCs may not be getting cheaper — £1,000 is still the entry point — but they are now much better value than they have ever been.

All new PCs are quite capable of making Windows 95 fly. If possible, buy something that is capable of a little more than you need right now. This will help keep the PC fresh for the next round of software upgrades and save you money and trouble in the long run.

Ideally, opt for a 15-inch digital monitor with the environment-friendly *EnergyStar* rating, as Windows 95 allows for low power standby and automatic shut-down modes. You'll also want a 16-bit sound card and 2Mb of video RAM.

Where possible, choose a Windows 95 keyboard.

This has three new keys for accessing the Start menu, pop-up menus and several shortcuts. While this is not a necessity it does enhance the Windows 95 system.

If you haven't yet bought your computer, or need help with the basics of computer-speak, I strongly recommend *The Complete Beginner's Guide to Buying and Using Your Computer* by Ewart Stronach. This guide will help get you up to speed with basic PC know-how using easy-to-understand language.

Printers and modems

While you don't have to buy a special printer or modem to work with Windows 95, it's worth watching for a label which reads "designed for Windows 95".

This indicates that the device supports the Plug-and-Play system — simply connect it to your PC and Windows 95 will automatically recognise the device and load the appropriate driver software. In some cases the device may come with its own disk of driver software which you will need to load through the Control Panel.

Is your PC ready for Windows 95?

Here's what I recommend for a workable Windows 95 system:

❑ CPU: minimum 486DX/2, aim for a 133MHz Pentium or higher.

❑ RAM: minimum 8Mb, aim for 16Mb or higher.

❑ Hard disk: minimum 540Mb, aim for 1.2Gb or higher.

❑ Monitor: minimum 14-inch, aim for 15-inch.

❑ Video: video card with 1Mb VRAM, aim for 2Mb.

❑ Sound card: 16-bit, SoundBlaster or SoundBlaster-compatible.

❑ CD-ROM: minimum double-speed drive, aim for four-speed or higher.

CHAPTER 5

Connecting Your Printer

Printing is a cinch in Windows 95. It's fast (especially using a laser printer) and, unlike other operating systems, the multitasking capabilities of Windows 95 let you continue to do other work while Windows is printing.

You'll find everything to do with printers in the Printers folder. You can access this from Control Panel (inside My Computer), or directly using the Settings folder in the Start menu.

Printers

This folder may also include an icon for Microsoft Fax. This isn't a printer as such — rather a way of sending faxes directly from Windows programs. Faxing is covered in more depth on page 46.

Setting up a printer

When you connect a printer to your PC and restart the system, Windows 95 will usually automatically detect it and load the appropriate printer driver (a small program that enables the PC and printer to talk to one another).

If that isn't the case, follow these steps to install any printer under Windows 95:

1. Open the Printers folder (either through Settings or My Computer) and double-click on the Add Printer icon.

2. Windows 95 works with almost 1000 printers — look through this list for yours. If a special Windows 95 driver disk was supplied with the printer click on the Have Disk button and follow the instructions.

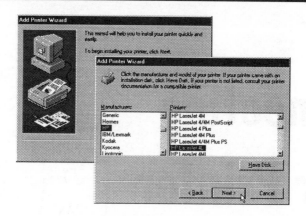

3. Windows prompts you to choose which "port" or connector on your PC the printer is hooked into. It's almost always LPT1.

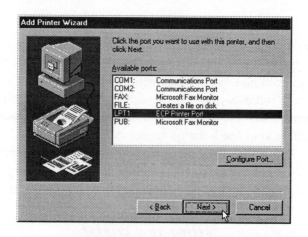

POWER TIP: PRINT TROUBLESHOOTER

Click on the Start menu, choose Help and open the Troubleshooting book. Click on the first entry, which is titled "If you have trouble printing...".

For heavy-duty help the Windows 95 CD-ROM contains an Enhanced Print Troubleshooter which you can copy to your PC. Simply insert the CD and use Windows Explorer to open the folder named Other. Inside this you'll find a folder named Misc, and inside this the folder named EPTS. If you have no luck here look through the manual that came with your printer, or, as a last resort, contact your computer repair store.

4. You can now rename the printer if you wish — Windows still knows which one you're talking about.

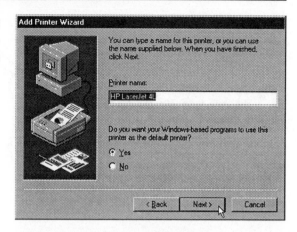

5. Print a test page and you're done! If you have a problem; Windows will run a Print Troubleshooter.

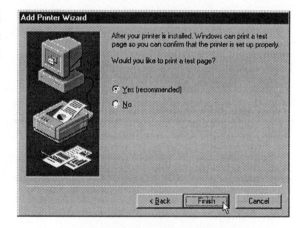

6. To change any printer settings, open the Printers folder, right-click on your printer and choose Properties.

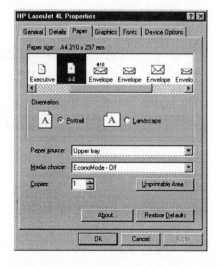

CHAPTER 6

Connecting Your Modem

Windows 95 lets you surf the Internet, send faxes, and tap into local computer bulletin boards. The first step to doing all of this is to connect your modem.

Actually, the first step is to *buy* a modem.

If you don't already have one of these clever gadgets I recommend an external fax modem (so you won't have to go fiddling with your PC's innards) running at a speed of 33.6Kbps. Look for a modem that's BT approved.

Modems

A fax modem is handy as it can send faxes, too — learn how to do this in out Ten Minute Tutor *Sending a Fax* on page 46.

Your modem handbook will advise how to connect the modem to your PC and, sometimes, how to install it under Windows 95. If not, here's what to do;

1. Open up the Control Panel and double-click on the Modems icon.

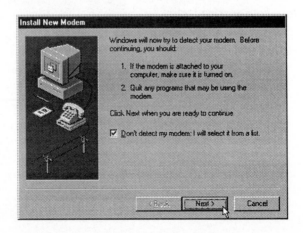

2. This runs the Install New Modem Wizard. Windows 95 can "auto-detect" the modem and (try to) choose the appropriate set-

QUICK TIP

If you're about to buy a modem, make sure it has been approved by BT.

ting, or you can tell Windows which modem you are using. Personally, I prefer to follow the latter course.

3. The list of modems which Windows 95 recognises is comprehensive, including both international and British manufacturers.

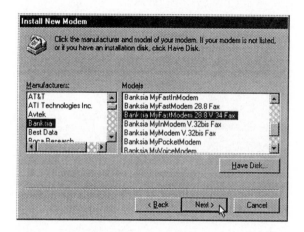

4. If your modem is not listed, look at the top of the list marked "Manufacturers for [Standard Modem Types]" and choose the speed in the Models list.

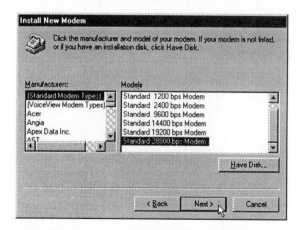

In either event, Windows will load the appropriate drivers and then prompt you to confirm which communications port to use. This is normally COM1.

> ## QUICK TIP
>
> *Some modems come with a disk of special 'driver' programs, designed to maximise efficiency under Windows 95. If you have these, click the Have Disk button and insert the disk into your floppy drive.*

5. Now Windows needs to know exactly where you'll be calling from. Enter your country and area code in the appropriate spaces, and check the type of phone system used.

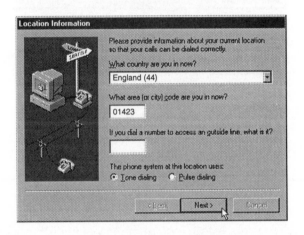

6. Next, configure the modem in the Modem Properties dialog box. Click on the Properties button to inspect the default settings.

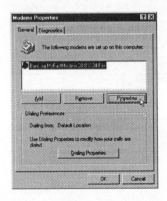

7. One setting you might want to check is Maximum Speed, which you'll find at the foot of the General tab.

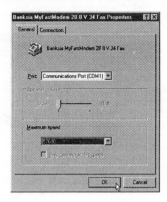

This is the "port speed" — the rate at which data is transferred between the PC and modem — and is independent of the actual modem speed. For a 14.4kbps modem set the Maximum Speed to 19200 or 38400; for a 28.8 Kbps or a 34.4Kbps modem use 57600.

8. Back at the Modem Properties dialog box the Dialling Properties sheet lets you set the parameters of your current location.

You won't need to change much here if you're using a desktop PC, but it's great for portable computing — you can set any number of locations such as home, office and hotel, with a different area code and outside line access numbers for each.

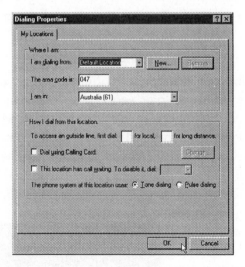

Hooray, now your modem is ready to go!

If at any time you decide to modify any setting, just run the Modems icon in the Control Panel and make the necessary changes — every Windows 95 program will recognise these changes next time you dial.

TEN MINUTE TUTOR

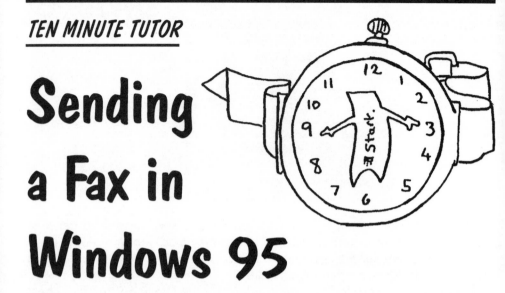

Sending a Fax in Windows 95

If you have a modem hooked up to your Windows 95 PC you've also got a fax machine sitting on your desktop!

That's right — everything you need to send and receive faxes is at your fingertips. You'll need to set up Windows 95 for faxing — but it won't be long before your first fax is speeding across the phone lines to its destination!

Introducing the Inbox

The Inbox icon on your Windows 95 desktop runs a program called Microsoft *Exchange* (in some later versions of Windows 95 this has been replaced by the faster but otherwise identical *Windows Messaging* utility).

Exchange is designed to handle all your Windows communications needs — from email (via *The Microsoft Network* and the Internet) to faxing.

You'll also find a Personal Address Book in *Exchange*. This is very handy for storing names, email addresses, fax numbers and contact information.

The first time you open the Inbox you'll be greeted by the Inbox Setup Wizard and asked which of the information services you wish to use.

For faxing, select Microsoft Fax by clicking in the box. Re-

QUICK TIP

Using the Inbox to receive faxes is not recommended. It's a clumsy procedure, as you'll be forever answering your phone to the squeals of a fax machine and rushing to turn on your PC.

move the check marks from The Microsoft Network Online Service and from Mail the same way, and then click on Next.

If a check-box for Microsoft Fax doesn't appear, you'll need to install this using the Add-Remove Software icon in the Control Panel.

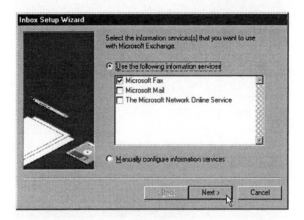

If you haven't yet set up your fax-modem, Windows 95 will let you do so now. If you already have a modem set up, click on Next.

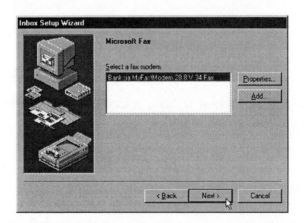

You'll now need to enter some information, such as your name and fax number, as well as creating a Personal Address Book and Personal Folders. You'll use the Address Book for names, email addresses and other contact information, and the folders to store faxes, emails, attached documents and so on. You can accept the default name and location for each file by clicking on Next.

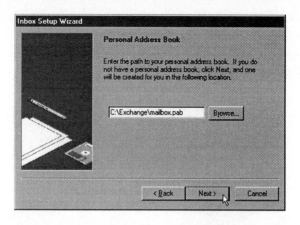

When you've finished, Exchange controls the Inbox, where you'll find a message waiting for you from Microsoft. Double-click on the message to read it.

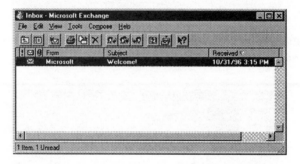

It's a good idea about now to have a look at the online Help, and learn more about the basics of the Inbox.

Sending a fax from the Inbox

Using the Inbox is a handy way to create simple one-page faxes — such as a quick note, a confirmation of a discussion or an order.

To do this, open your Inbox and configure Microsoft *Fax* by choosing, in turn, Tools, Microsoft Fax Tools, and Options.

Don't forget to enter your own details on the User tab, as these will automatically fill fields on the cover sheet.

Now, select Compose, followed by New Fax. This creates a single-page text-based fax.

If you have a more complex message to send choose New Message, which allows you to create pictures and charts in WordPad — then simply fax the WordPad document.

When you've finished composing your fax, clicking on New Fax calls up another Wizard to help you on your way!

Enter the recipient's details straight onto this screen, or select them from your Address Book.

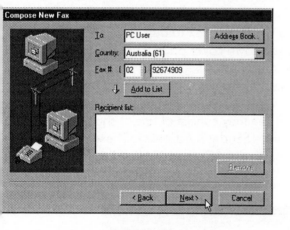

Now, all that's left is to select a cover page, add any comments, and leave it to the Wizard to send the fax via your fax-modem.

Sending a fax from an application

Using Windows 95, faxing a document prepared in an application is as simple as printing it.

Choose Print on the File menu, then select Microsoft Fax from the drop-down Printer Name list.

This sends the page(s) to your fax-modem, runs a Wizard to prompt you for an address and cover sheet, and dispatches the fax.

Designing a cover page

The Windows 95 "Cover Page Editor" allows you to create any number of cover pages for home or business use. You can totally customise your faxes by adding personal artwork, text and layout.

Try it out for yourself: click the Start button, choose the Programs folder, then the Accessories folder and finally the Fax folder.

For ideas on how to design your own cover page, click the File menu and choose Open, and look inside the Windows folder at the four cover pages supplied with Windows 95: they're named Confidential, Urgent, Generic and For Your Information.

Open any of these and you'll see they consist of lots of shapes containing names like {Recipient Name} and {Sender's Address}. These are automatically filled in using data entered in the "Compose New Fax Wizard" or in your Address Book.

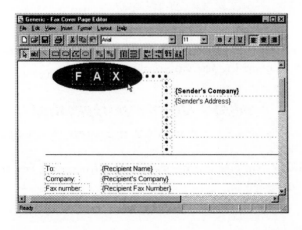

Using the Address Book

The Inbox Address Book is a handy little device which saves you the time (and finger-work) needed to address faxes to numbers you use frequently.

The Address book also allows you to record other information (such as company name, postal address and phone numbers).

Programs such as Microsoft *Word for Windows* can use this data to address individual letters or to perform what is known as a "mail merge" — sending the same letter to a number of people, but with each letter customised to include a specific name and address.

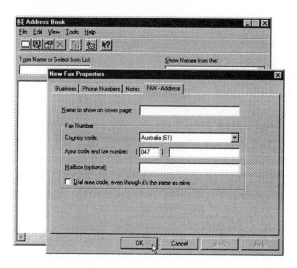

QUICK TIP

In all honesty, the powerful Inbox is an overkill for sending a simple fax — I don't recommend it unless your PC has 16Mb of RAM. The problem is that the next best software, Symantec's WinFax Pro 7.5, also needs 16Mb of memory. Maybe you'd better get 16Mb and be done with it...!

CHAPTER 7

Windows on the World

It's almost certain that you've heard about the Internet, either in a computer magazine, from a PC-literate friend, or through the newspapers or TV. It's just as likely that you're confused by exactly what the Internet is — and, more importantly, just what it has to offer you.

The Internet is a vast, sprawling mass of computers — tens of millions of them, ranging from desktop PCs to large university and corporate "mainframes". These are all interconnected, like the strands of a spider's web, so that any one computer can share information with another.

The beauty of the Internet is that it belongs to everyone — quite literally so, because no government or corporation "owns" the Internet. Because of this you'll find the content of the Net as diverse as humanity itself.

What can you do on the Net? Almost anything!

For example, you can communicate with other people using private electronic mail (called *email*). Imagine the advantages of being able to instantly (or near-instantly) send written communication to a friend, a relative or even a business contact. Just type in your message, hit the Send button and it's away, travelling across the Internet to its destination anywhere in the world.

The World Wide Web is the most exciting part of the Internet.

On the Web you can view wonderfully colourful "pages" which work just like Windows software — click on an icon or highlighted text (called a hyperlink) and you'll be connected to a related screen of information.

The Web spans the globe, which means that at the click of a mouse button you can access computers throughout the world — visit a London museum one minute, and a French university the next.

The best bit is that Web pages include glorious colourful pictures as well as text. They can also contain sound and video clips which you can play on your PC screen while you're connected or "download" them (transfer across the phone line onto your computer) to use anytime you choose.

On the Web you'll find software and information on just about any topic of interest: from the latest news and sports results, to hobbies, education, research and business.

In a *Newsgroup* you can swap written comments, notes, tips, questions, answers, jokes and more, with people who share your interests.

These discussion groups cover almost every possible interest, from hobbies to professional subjects: art, books, cars, education, food, genealogy, home-brewing, literature, movies, gardening, music, politics, science, sport and (of course) computers

You can also talk (well, "type" to be more accurate) live to anyone else on the Net using *Internet Relay Chat*.

This means that as you type a message to your computer, it appears on the screen of the person you are "chatting" to, and vice-versa.

There are chat "channels" for any topic you care to mention, and it's a real buzz to sit in front of your PC exchanging messages with someone who could as easily be in the next room as in Alaska.

And who said that the Internet is all work and no play? Via interactive games you can join other players online to discover new worlds, such as Fantasy Worlds at http://www.real virtual.com/fantasyworlds. html.

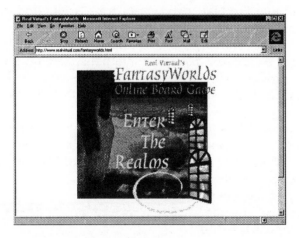

File transfer protocol (FTP) enables you to fetch computer files from other computers on the Internet. Just locate the file you want and it can be transferred directly to your own PC.

What do I need to get connected?

To get hooked up you'll need three things (besides your computer, of course):

❑ **A modem**, which sits between your PC and the phone line. All you need to know for now is that your modem should be fast. In modem terms "fast" means it should shovel data down the phone line at a speed of

33,600 bits per second — which is referred to as 33,600bps or "33.6K" (the K means "one thousand"). See chapter 6 "Connecting your modem" for more on modems.

❑ **Access to the Internet.** You'll need to sign up with a company called an "Internet service provider" (ISP) through which you can connect to the Internet. There is usually a one-off registration fee, as well as an hourly charge for the time you spend "online". We have a special Internet access offer for readers of this guide on page 128.

❑ Special (mostly free) **Internet software** — including a "Web browser" for zooming around the World Wide Web, and an "email client" for sending and receiving electronic mail.

If you want to learn more about the Internet, I suggest Mark Neely's *Complete Beginner's Guide to the Internet* which will tell you all about the Internet, as well as weird and wonderful places you can surf to.

Loading Windows 95's Internet system

Most ISPs will supply you with a "starter kit" of software which automatically installs the necessary Internet software and configures your Windows PC to dial into the Net. This hassle-free "smile and dial" approach is by far the best route.

If your local ISP is unable to provide such a package, however, follow these steps to get Windows 95's inbuilt Internet system up and running.

1. If you've previously installed any Internet software, locate and disable its WINSOCK.DLL, which may conflict with the one bundled with Windows 95.

Use the Windows 95 Find feature (located on the Start menu) to search your entire hard drive for any file named WINSOCK.DLL. Keep the file in the WINDOWS or WINDOWS\SYSTEM directory (don't panic if it's in both) dated 11/07/95 and 42Kb in size.

Rename any of the others by right-clicking on the file, choosing Rename from the pop-up menu and typing in a name (such as WINSOCK.OLD).

2. A typical installation of Windows 95 doesn't include the Dial-Up Networking applet (mini-application) used to establish a connection with your ISP.

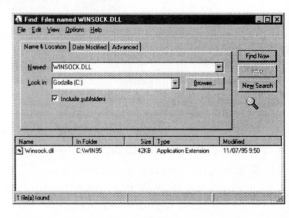

Understanding the World Wide Web

(A) The 'home page' is where you start every Internet session.

(B) Click here to access a 'search engine' — a special Internet site which can find Web pages containing key words or phrases.

(C) When you discover an interesting Web site, add it to your Favourites folder so you can visit it again just by clicking this menu.

(D) Click here to send electronic mail or 'email' across the Net.

(E) Microsoft Internet Explorer lets you add single-click links to the sites you visit most often.

(F) This is the 'URL' or address of the current Web page.

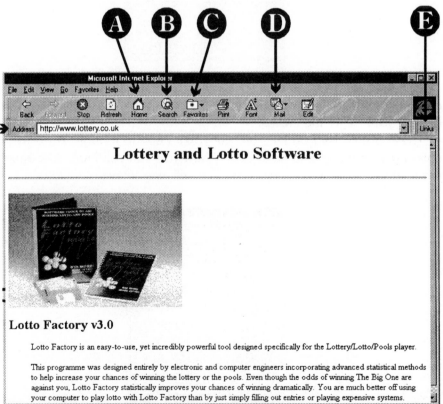

If there's a Dial-Up Networking folder inside your desktop's My Computer icon, go to step 3. If not, you'll need to add it yourself. To do this open the Control Panel and choose the Add/Remove Programs utility.

Click on the Windows Setup tab, and from the Components list choose Communications, then click on the Details button. Now check the Dial-Up Networking box and click on OK.

To load these components you'll need to feed the Windows 95 CD-ROM or floppy disks.

A curiosity is that because Windows 95 treats the Internet like any other computer network, you are prompted for unique names which would usually identify your PC in the crowd.

These aren't used on the Net, but you'll need to indulge Windows 95 by entering something into each box before you can continue. Just enter anything which takes your fancy — no one will ever know!

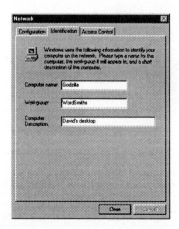

3. Dial-Up Networking also installs a selection of basic network components. These can be viewed by clicking on the Configuration tab in the Network dialog box. This dialog box is where you'll configure your Windows 95
system for all network access, including access to the Internet.

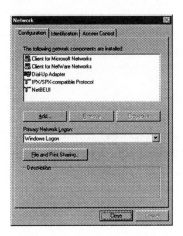

To reach this dialog box at any time, open the Control Panel and select the
Network icon.

Begin configuring by getting rid of excess baggage. If your PC is not
part of a network (and you won't be dialling into an office LAN) select
Client for Microsoft Networks and click on Remove. Repeat this until all
that remains is Dial-Up Adaptor. If at some stage you do set up a computer network at the office or even in the home (don't laugh, many of my
friends are "networking" their PC with the old machine in the kids' room!)
you can easily restore these settings.

Now you need to add
something to the mix: a computer language or "protocol"
called TCP/IP. This is the digital tongue spoken by all
computers on the Internet.

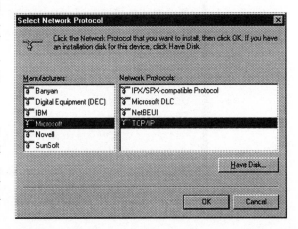

Click on the Add button
and, in the Select Network
Component Type dialog box,
choose Protocol, then select
Add. In the Manufacturers list

box select Microsoft (the people who wrote Windows 95) and from the Network Protocols list box choose TCP/IP, then click on OK.

4. Back in the Network dialog box select Dial-Up Adaptor, then click on Properties and, under the Bindings tab, ensure that TCP/IP is selected. Now return to the Network dialog, select TCP/IP and click on the Properties button.

At this point you'll need to obtain a complete set of instructions from your Internet service provider: there are usually special numbers and settings (some unique to each ISP) which must be one hundred per cent right to successfully connect.

Internet software

Now all you need are the Windows applications needed to tour the World Wide Web, send and receive email and so on. Turn to chapter 9, *The best of Windows 95 software* for my favourites and recommendations.

NIFTY NETWARE

One of the best things about the Net is the free software out there, ready to download. These URLs will take you to some of the nifty software you'll find mentioned in this guide.
Eudora Lite (version 1.54):
http://www.eudora.com/light.html#download
Microsoft Internet Mail & News:
http://www.microsoft.com/msdownload/ieadd/14000.htm
FreeAgent 1.1:
http://www.forteinc.com/getfa/download.htm
Symantec Internet Fast Find (trial version):
http://www.symantec.com/cgi-bin/downloadiffbeta.pl

TEN MINUTE TUTOR

Using the Recycle Bin

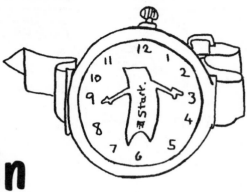

When you delete a file or folder in Windows 95, either by choosing Delete in Windows Explorer or dropping the item into the Recycle Bin, it isn't really removed from your hard drive. Yes, it disappears from view. But Windows actually moves it to a special hidden folder called "Recycled", where it is stored until you decide either to undelete it or remove it for good. The Recycle Bin is the user-friendly face of this mechanism.

You'll find the Recycle Bin on your desktop. Double-clicking on it opens a folder window containing files which have been deleted.

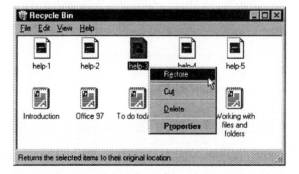

If you wish to undelete a file, simply select it, right-click, and then choose Restore from the pop-up menu — this will return it to the location from which it was deleted. Easy!

Warning: *Files and folders which are deleted from floppy disks, from inside programs and at the MS-DOS prompt bypass the Recycle Bin entirely. The only way to restore these files is by using* Norton Utilities 95.

When the Recycle Bin is viewed in Details mode you will notice two columns entitled Original Location and Date Deleted.

POWER TIP: CALLING DR NORTON

Yikes!

Yesterday you deleted a file, this morning you emptied the Recycle Bin — and now, of course, you desperately need that very file!

As far as Windows is concerned your file is gone, full stop. But if you have Norton Utilities for Windows 95 you can use Norton's UnErase Wizard to recover your handiwork (although even Norton can't work

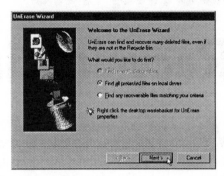

miracles and resurrect long-lost files). This aspect of the program alone makes it worth buying!

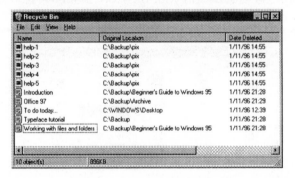

Clicking on a column header sorts files in the Recycle Bin according to that criteria — making it simple to identify a file which you recall deleting two days ago or from a particular folder.

Because files in the Recycle Bin aren't in fact deleted, they occupy just as much space as if they were still on your hard drive (which they actually are). To free up this

QUICK TIP

If you want to make sure no-one can recover a file or folder from your Recycle Bin, hold down the Shift key while you drag it into the Bin. This immediately sends the object into oblivion.

space, right-click on the Recycle Bin icon (or pull down the File menu inside the Recycle Bin folder) and choose Empty Recycle Bin.

Recycle Bin

You can choose the amount of space set aside for the Recycle Bin, and disable the dialog box which asks you to confirm each file deletion — see chapter 10, *Doing Windows Your Way* for more information.

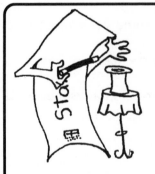

POWER TIP: THE RECYCLE BIN ICON

If you're tired of looking at the same old Recycle Bin icon each day, try the shareware program MicroAngelo (included in our shareware offer at the back of this book). This marvellous icon workshop lets you replace the standard Bin with any icon you fancy. My favourite icon is a box of floppy disks, one of the many desktop delights which comes with the Microsoft Plus pack. I've also seen toilets, dumpster bins, nuclear reactors . . .

CHAPTER 8

Win 95 Software

Among the most-asked questions about Windows 95 is: "Do I need new software?".

The answer, as a rule, is no.

Most programs designed for Windows 3.x and even MS-DOS will run well under Windows 95 — sometimes much better than in their native environment.

However, there are certain cautions, as well as some good reasons to make a switch to dedicated Windows 95 software.

To discuss this issue, the term "software" will be divided into three sections:

- ❏ **Applications** (programs such as wordprocessors, spreadsheets and desktop publishing, as well as reference CD-ROMs);
- ❏ **Games**; and
- ❏ **"Utility"** programs.

Applications

Not **all** old application programs are guaranteed to perform flawlessly under Windows 95.

When designing their new operating system, Microsoft had to make a choice: either build a completely new platform requiring users to buy all new programs (a decision which would have meant financial suicide); or maintain a degree of compatibility with software written in the days of MS-DOS and Windows 3.1. In effect, Windows 95 is a compromise between the best of the new and old worlds.

Most Windows 3.x applications run smooth as silk under Windows 95, although some programs — among them *WordPerfect 6.1 for Windows* — may experience a range of difficulties. The behaviour of DOS applications is even harder to predict.

Microsoft has released a "Software Compatibility Report" which details the interaction of Windows 95 with hundreds of common programs. This can be found on its Web page at www.microsoft.com/WindowsSupport/.

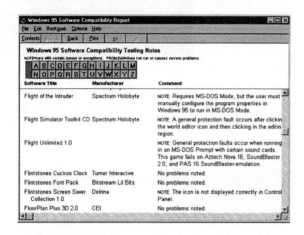

The disadvantage of Windows 3.x applications is in their handling of files and folders. Names must conform to the 8.3 specification, and long file names are automatically shortened.

Windows 3.x applications also don't allow you to save documents on the Windows 95 desktop — a handy resting place for day-to-day work. Instead of simply clicking on the Desktop (in the File Save dialog box), files must be saved in the directory which is called C:\WINDOWS\DESKTOP.

Games

Running Windows 3.x games under Windows 95 can prove problematic.

Most games are designed to run under MS-DOS, and pre-Windows 95 releases (such as the *Doom* and *Descent* series) load their own memory management software, graphical display engines and drivers — modules which can conflict with the equivalent Windows 95 controllers. Launching such a game from Windows 95 may cause it to run erratically — it might freeze for several seconds (a lethal flaw in action epics like *Doom*), or cease working.

There are two ways around this.

The first is to choose Shut Down from the Windows 95 Start menu, and then select "Restart the computer in MS-DOS mode". This suspends Windows 95 and returns you to the DOS prompt from where you can run your game (this approach may also work for troublesome DOS applications). When you've finished the game type EXIT or WIN at the DOS prompt and Windows will restart without rebooting.

The second option is to select "MS-DOS Prompt" from the Programs folder (in the Start menu). This differs from the previous procedure, as the prompt merely initiates a DOS session in a new window (leaving Windows 95 running in the background). This is useful if you want to switch between DOS and Windows applications.

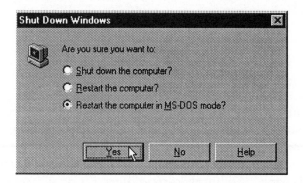

If you have kept an earlier version of DOS on your PC (such as MS-DOS 6.22) you have a third alternative for accessing pre-Windows 95 games. When you switch on your PC and see the screen message "Starting Windows 95", press the F4 key. This bypasses Windows 95 entirely, and loads the original MS-DOS on your PC.

Utilities

Utilities are tools which safeguard your data, keep your hardware in tip-top shape and make it easier to manage your files. File managers such as *Xtree* and *Norton Commander*, interface improvers like *Norton Desktop*, disk tools such as *Norton Utilities* and anti-virus programs all fall under this heading.

Don't even try running utilities built for MS-DOS or Windows 3.x under Windows 95. These have been written to suit the 16-bit architecture of DOS and Windows 3.x, rather than the re-designed 32-bit firmament of Windows 95. The result could be irreparable damage to your data.

Utilities are the one part of your software library which you *must* upgrade when choosing Windows 95.

Why buy Windows 95 software?

Windows 95 programs — applications, utilities and games alike — are designed to take full advantage of the power of your computer.

Almost all Windows 3.1 programs are written using 16-bit code, and, while they run noticeably faster in Windows 95 (due to superior handling of memory and system resources) they are still noticeably outperformed by the 32-bit Windows 95 programs.

Most Windows 95 programs are more reliable than older programs, too. They use less memory and allow you to multitask (switch between several programs and operations at once).

Other advantages include the ability to use long file and folder names, to drag-and-drop files to and from the desktop, and an Uninstall feature which can quickly and effectively remove all traces of a program.

Look for the logo

How do you know if a program is built for Windows 95?

Keep an eye out for a "Designed for Windows 95" sticker on the box. This signifies that the program has met the qualifications set by Microsoft — full 32-bit code, support for long filenames, multitasking, and an uninstall routine among others.

But beware — software advertised as "Runs under Windows 95" or "Works with Windows 95" is NOT the same as that designed for Windows 95. You may be paying for a 16-bit program dressed up in 32-bit clothing.

The whys and wherefores of wares . . .

Windows software comes in four basic flavours: commercial software; shareware; freeware; and trialware.

Commercial software is bought over the counter. You hand over money in return for a big shrink-wrapped box, containing some slim manuals and a single CD. The product may be great — but what a waste of packaging and shelf space! And you may even take it home to discover that it's not exactly what you wanted.

Shareware is software which is distributed on a "try-

QUICK TIP

You can purchase shareware from many newsagents, computer stores and magazines, including this one, but the price only covers packaging and distribution. It doesn't include registration. That's up to you — provided you like the program and want to keep using it legally.

before-you-buy" basis. You can use the program for free before deciding if you want to register it by sending a modest payment to the author or agent.

There is usually no limit on the amount of time you can use the program before you decide to pay for it, and the "computer-police" won't hunt you down if you never do.

However, registering shareware keeps it alive, and the benefits of this to computer users are obvious. Often, to encourage payment, the registered version includes additional features or manuals.

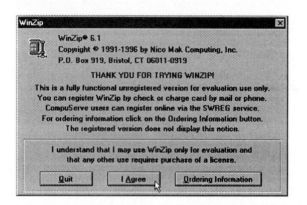

Freeware or "public domain software" is, as its name indicates, totally free.

This doesn't mean that freeware is worthless. Some of the best software in my toolkit is freeware. Freeware is written by people who — believe it or not — write software purely for the fun of it!

One twist on this concept is "postcardware". In return for using the program the programmers ask you to send a picture postcard from your home town — just to show how much their efforts are appreciated!

Trialware is being distributed by a growing number of companies via the Internet.

This is a fully functional edition of a commercial program which can be used for a trial period (usually 30 days). At the end of this time the program stops working.

The aim of trialware is to have you so hooked on the software by the end of the trial period that you'll buy the commercial version.

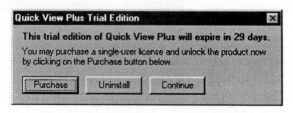

Installing Windows 95 software

When it comes to both loading and removing software from your computer, Windows 95 has excellent manners. Most programs feature Setup Wizards which take you step-by-step through the installation process.

To install software which is on CD-ROM, simply insert the CD into your computer. A setup screen will appear — from here you can begin the installation routine.

If your software is supplied on floppy disks, open Control Panel and choose Add/Remove Programs, then click on the Install button under the Install/Uninstall tab. Windows will take care of the rest.

At some stage you may want to remove software from your system.

To do this, simply open the Control Panel, choose Add/Remove Programs and click on the Install/Uninstall tab. Scroll through the list of installed programs below the Recycle Bin icon, then select the name of the program to be removed and click on the Add/Remove button.

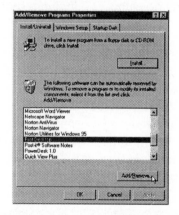

CHAPTER 9

The Best of Windows 95 Software

M ost new software is designed for Windows 95. Here's my list of commercial programs that I can't do without — try them and you'll be hooked!

Wordprocessing

Microsoft *Word for Windows* is the world's most popular wordprocessor for Windows 95: slick, packed with power and hand-holding "wizards" (just like those in Windows 95 itself).

The changing face of *Word* provides a good illustration of the differences between 16-bit and 32-bit versions of a Windows application, as well as the evolution of software under the influence of Windows 95.

Word 6.0 on Windows 3.1: Shown below, this is undoubtedly an attractive wordprocessor, although names are restricted to eight characters.

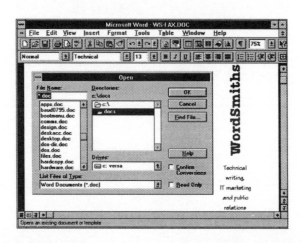

Word 6.0 on Windows 95: The 16-bit *Word 6* gets an instant face-lift under Windows 95, but beauty is only skin deep — long files and folder names are still cut short.

However, this is the only significant failing: *Word 6* under Windows 95 (shown right) runs better than on its native Windows 3.1 platform.

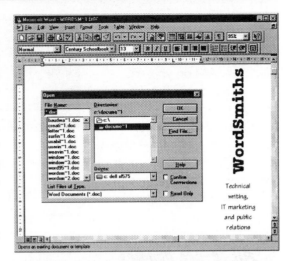

Word 95 on Windows 95: Built for Windows 95, *Word 95* (shown right) is faster and better-looking than previous versions.

Long file and directory names are supported, and the File, Open dialog box contains handy tools for finding and managing documents. If you have 16Mb of RAM you'll do best with *Word 95* (part of the *Office 95* family).

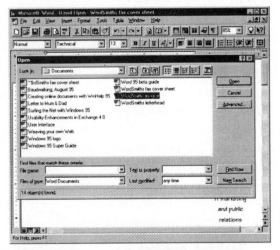

Word 97 on Windows 95: Take a good look at *Word 97*, the latest version of *Word* which is bundled as part of Microsoft's *Office 97* pack. The menus and toolbars have a more chiselled appearance, new features include the "document map" and on-the-fly grammar checker (shown right), plus a 3D drawing module and World Wide Web page authoring program.

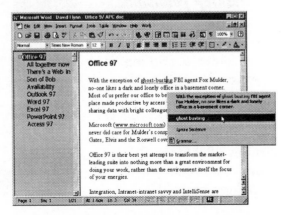

Word 97 is my word-crafting tool of choice, although I recommend it only if you have 32Mb of RAM on your PC.

If Word doesn't take your fancy, consider Corel WordPerfect 7.0. This Windows 95 version of the champion DOS program outstrips Microsoft Word when it comes to handling tables, layout and graphics.

All-in-one bundles

For little more than the price of a wordprocessor you can often buy an integrated collection of essential business applications, which may include a wordprocessor, spreadsheet, presentation program, personal information organiser and database. The best value bundles are Microsoft Office 97, Office 95 and Corel WordPerfect Suite 7.0.

A package just right for home use is Microsoft Works 95. This is essentially a low-calorie version of Office, with a wordprocessor, spreadsheet, database and charting program rolled into one. Works is often included with new PCs.

Desktop publishing

For modest home and business needs Microsoft Publisher comes out on top.

An array of Wizards and templates provide ready-made publications — all you need to add is words and pictures. Publisher 97 even helps you design World Wide Web pages.

> ### QUICK TIP
>
> Documents created in Word 97 can't be read by Word 95 without installing a special file converter (supplied with Word 97). However, these programs do share the same document format, however.

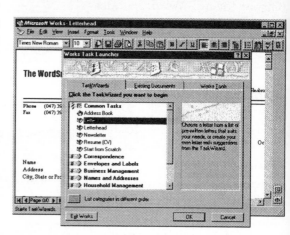

At the opposite end of the spectrum lie *Adobe PageMaker* and *Quark Xpress*. These hi-tech programs are used to craft those polished, glossy publications such as magazines and catalogues. Most home or home-office users will find that the capabilities of these programs far exceed their needs.

Drawing

For affordable all-in-one graphics muscle I recommend the Corel *Graphics Pack* — a fantastic bundle of graphics applications which can tackle any task.

Users who really want to stretch both their creativity and their Windows 95 PC to the limit will find *CorelDRAW! 7.0* unbeatable — although this high-end program has more to offer than most home users will ever need.

Micrografx *Windows Draw 4.0* and *Draw 5.0* are an impressive package, capable of everything that the home or business user could demand, such as certificates, invitations, calendars, stationery, family trees and flowcharts.

Draw includes over 150 templates for instant results, plus 10,000 clip art images and 250 TrueType fonts.

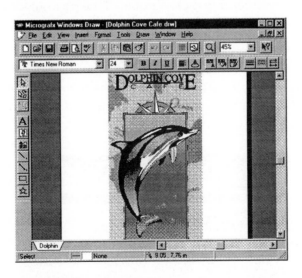

Visio 4.0 is aimed at the corporate user and advanced small office. This award-winning program firmly targets "business diagramming".

Using *Visio* you drag shapes (such as engineering, office design and computer network glyphs) from a stencil palette to create flowcharts, graphs and other business artwork, as shown in the following screenshot.

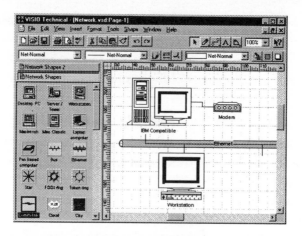

Personal finance

Microsoft *Money* and Intuit *Quicken* are designed to help manage your home budget. Both these programs will track income and expenses, balance cheque books and calculate the value of your investments — then present the good (or bad) news in a simple table or chart.

     Quicken is the smarter and more flexible of the pair but lacks the snappier interface and user guidance of Money.

Internet

The World Wide Web is the star attraction of the Internet. You'll need a piece of software called a Web browser to get there, and your choice is between Netscape *Navigator* and Microsoft *Internet Explorer*.

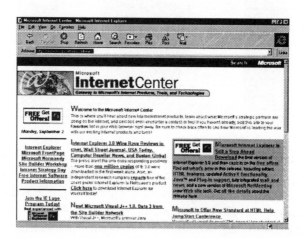

My personal favourite is *Internet Explorer*. It's only marginally faster than *Netscape* but substantially easier to use.

You can customise the interface, apply a rudimentary parental lock to keep the kids away from sites with undesirable or pornographic content, and store your most-visited Web pages in a drop-down favourites list.

> ## QUICK TIP
>
> *What to do with your old software? Why not donate it to your local school, church, or community organisation? Many of these groups can't afford the latest software and will welcome your gift.*

Mind you, the race between Microsoft and Netscape for supremacy in this market is hotly contested and each company strives to outdo the other with successive versions of their browser. There is unlikely to be a definitive champion for some time to come.

Microsoft's Windows 95 *Plus Pack* CD-ROM includes the primitive *Internet Explorer 1.0* — this will at least get you on the Net, where you can download the latest version for free.

Electronic mail (email) is the new way to communicate. It's faster, simpler and cheaper than a letter or a fax.

Microsoft *Internet Explorer 3.0* comes with Microsoft *Internet Mail 1.0*, and it's all you need to join the email revolution.

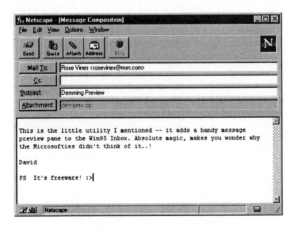

You can also access email using the *Navigator Mail* module in *Netscape Navigator 3.0*, or the free stand-alone program *Eudora Lite*. You can download version 1.54 of Eudora from the Internet, using the URL supplied on page 73.

If you have Microsoft *Office 97* try the email module of the *Outlook 97* information manager.

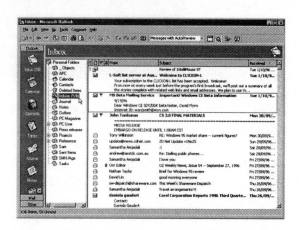

Via newsgroups you can discuss almost any topic — but to join in you'll need a newsgroup reader.

You'll find useful newsgroup readers in both *Internet Explorer* and *Netscape Navigator*, although the best is the freeware program *FreeAgent 1.1* from Forte.

Symantec also produce a winning collection of commercial Internet utilities under the banner of *Internet FastFind*.

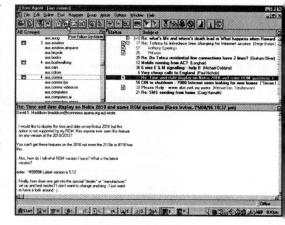

Desktop accessories

Quick View Plus is an extension of the *Quick View* applet bundled with Windows 95. It allows you to view over 200 wordprocessor, spreadsheet, database, graphics and Internet file types without having to open the file in an application.

With *Quick View Plus* you can also print the document, search for text, and copy selected text or graphics to the Clipboard.

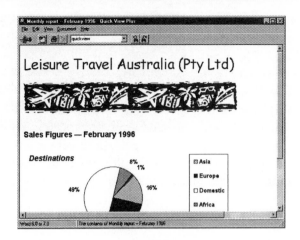

Utilities

Symantec's *Norton Utilities 95* is a wiz at solving software conflicts, recovering erased files (even if you've already emptied the Recycle Bin), preventing unexpected program shutdowns and restoring crashed systems.

It includes powerful versions of the Windows 95 disk defragmenter and scanner to maximise performance and prolong disk life. The handy System Doctor monitors your PC's vital signs and warns you of impending problems.

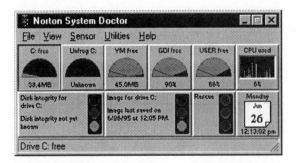

Symantec's *Healthy PC* is a lighter-weight utility, but still quite capable of performing a complete PC-maintenance check of your system, fixing disk errors and removing viruses — all at the click of a mouse button.

If you're looking for convenience, *Norton Navigator* includes several very handy tools for Windows 95.

QuickMenus, for example, display the contents of folders nested several levels deep, enabling you to drill down to any level without having to actually open each successive folder.

Norton File Manager is a vast improvement over Windows 95 Explorer. File management commands are added to the File Open and File Save dialog boxes of all Windows 95 applications.

> ## QUICK TIP
>
> *If you buy Norton Utilities for Windows 95, be sure to get version 2.0. Since its release Windows 95 has undergone some significant changes, and Norton 2.0 was designed with these in mind.*

Users can also set up multiple "desktops", each with a unique set of folders and objects required for a particular task, to keep their normal workaday desktop free from icon overload.

Anti-virus

Norton Anti-Virus has saved my bacon (and my data) many times over — and continues to do so with virus updates posted on the Internet each month.

Other leading virus sentries include *PC-cillin*, *VET* and McAfee's *Scan*. Choose any of these products, but don't run your PC without one of them.

File transfer

If you need to shift files between PCs, you can't go wrong with *LapLink 95*.

This program supports the usual desktop/portable computer partnership, but also excels at modem connections. Using *Laplink* you can access the hard drive of a "remote" machine to transfer files or even run programs. It's fast, simple and almost foolproof.

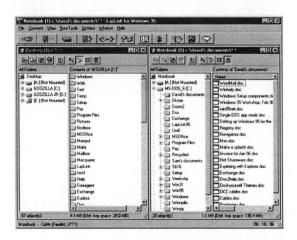

Faxing

The built-in fax sub-system of Windows 95 has helped take the fiddle out of faxing — but it's not without limits. For industrial-strength faxing you need Delrina *WinFax PRO 7.5*.

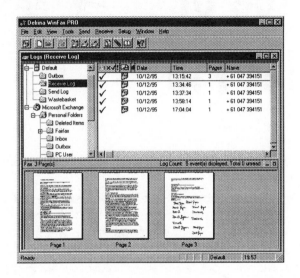

Use the Send Fax wizard to fire-off a basic cover page, choose one of the hundreds of pre-designed cover sheets, or create your own with the Cover Page Designer. Fax transmissions can be scheduled or noted as recurring events — handy for sending daily or weekly reports.

WinFax PRO receives faxes too, and can also automatically display, print or convert a received fax into editable text which can be simply opened as a wordprocessing document.

CHAPTER 10

A Slice of Applet Pie

Windows 95 comes with a handful of little applications, sometimes called applets.

You'll still need to buy some off-the-shelf software to get any real work done, but these desktop accessories are useful for daily tasks. They'll also get you used to the way things work in Windows 95, so when you step up to the higher-end programs you'll already know the basics.

You'll find the Windows applets in the Accessories file in the Start menu.

Notepad

This is Windows' equivalent of a shorthand jotter.

Notepad does not allow formatting, so you can't select a font or make text bold or italic. About all you can do is create a quick note, save it or print it.

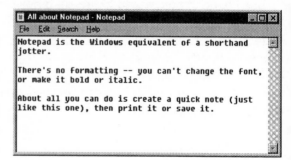

All about Notepad - Notepad

File Edit Search Help

Notepad is the Windows equivalent of a shorthand jotter.

There's no formatting -- you can't change the font, or make it bold or italic.

About all you can do is create a quick note (just like this one), then print it or save it.

QUICK TIP

Notepad includes two handy features. To insert the current time and date into a document hit F5. And, if you want to stop lines running past the edge of the window, choose Wordwrap from the Edit menu.

WordPad

WordPad is just the trick for quick memos, letters, and to-do lists.

Wordpad's capabilities are fairly comprehensive, sharing the basic features of

Microsoft's *Word for Windows* wordprocessor — including text formatting, icon toolbars, and a print preview (which shows a thumbnail image of the page as it will print).

Paint

You don't have to be an artist to use Paint.

This is a simple doodling tool with a variety of brushes, colours and effects. Kids can spend hours dabbling in Paint and really keen users can use it to design simple artwork.

For professional results, however, you'll need something with a little more power, like the graphics program COREL*Draw!*

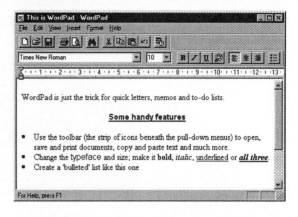

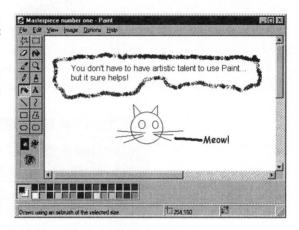

Quick View

Quick View lets you see the contents of many wordprocessing, spreadsheet and graphic files without actually opening the file in the application which created it.

You don't need to fire up a large wordprocessing program or even own one to read a document — just right-click on a file and, if the file type is supported, select the Quick View option in the pop-up menu.

Phone Dialer

Connect a modem to your PC and this great little applet will let you dial phone numbers from your Windows 95 desktop

Eight favourite numbers can be entered into "Speed dial".

CD Player

The Windows 95 CD Player (which you'll find in the Multimedia folder within Accessories) allows you to listen to your favourite audio CDs while you work.

Options include random play, programmable playback order and the ability to save a "play list" for any disc, so you hear only the tracks you want.

Calculator

Now you'll never have to go digging around your desk drawer looking for a pocket calculator when it's time to tally up all those figures!

The Windows Calculator has two faces: in standard guise it's a basic number cruncher with a memory — but pull down the View menu and it becomes a complete scientific calculator, perfect for anyone involved with maths, engineering, statistics or physics.

Character Map

Use the Character Map to insert special characters into wordprocessors such as WordPad.

Windows 95 comes with the Wingdings and Symbol fonts already loaded. These contain a wide array of scientific notation, foreign language characters, arrows and even some tiny pieces of art to brighten the dullest document.

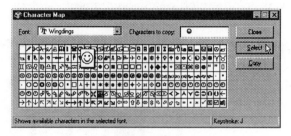

Briefcase

The Briefcase is designed for people who need to work on the same files using different computers — maybe one at the office and another at home.

Drop these documents and reports into the Briefcase, then simply copy the Briefcase onto a floppy disk.

Insert this disk into another PC, "open" the Briefcase — and your files are instantly accessible!

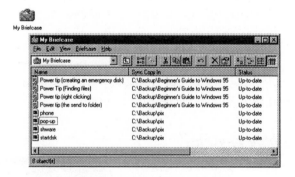

Lights, camera, action!

Windows 95 includes several applets which showcase its ability to handle multimedia content, such as sound and video clips. Some sample files are loaded into your Windows folder and more can be found in the "Funstuff" folder on your Windows 95 CD-ROM.

Does this mean you could watch a movie on your PC?

Well, yes — except that the view is limited to a very small window and video files are so large that a feature film would occupy a whole 1Gb hard drive!

But of course, nothing stays the same forever. A new CD-ROM format called DVD can store whole movies, audio CDs, plus interactive games on a single disc. Moves are also underway to establish a "PC-TV" standard which can display computer images, TV shows, movie pictures and the Internet on a single device with a large high-definition monitor.

Games people play

This roll-call of productivity may give you the impression that Windows 95 is all work and no play. Not so. Pop up the Start menu, open the Programs folder, then select the Accessories and open Games.

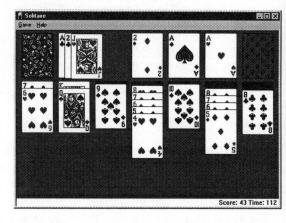

Solitaire is a computerised version of this classic solo card game. It's quite addictive — but as you're playing you're also learning essential Windows skills such as clicking, dragging and dropping.

FreeCell and Hearts are card games modelled on their real-world counterparts.

Winning at Minesweeper takes equal portions of logic and chance. Tension mounts as you click on each square to uncover safe territory, an indication of how many mines are in the surrounding squares or — if you're unlucky — you'll find that you've clicked on a mine!

Something missing?

If any of these accessories doesn't appear on your Start menu, simply install them from your Windows 95 CD-ROM.

Open the Control Panel and click on the Add/Remove Programs icon. Click on the tab labelled "Windows Setup". Highlight Accessories, click on the Details button and select the missing components. Then click on OK.

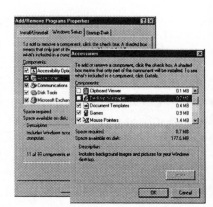

TEN MINUTE TUTOR

Fantastic Fonts

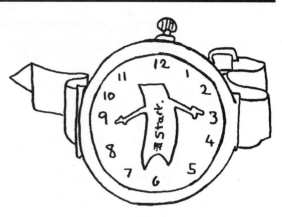

Fonts, sometimes called typefaces, are the clothes which letters and numbers wear. The words you're reading now have been formatted with the Futura font. The headings and subheadings use the DomCasual typeface.

Before the introduction of Windows-based wordprocessing, formatting changes were shown on screen only as changes in display. Bold type, for example, would be shown in blue, italics in green and so on.

Windows introduced WYSIWYG ("What You See Is What You Get") which means that you can "paint" a newsletter or memo in your wordprocessor with a particular font and see exactly how it will appear when printed.

A selection of TrueType fonts are loaded when you install Windows 95.

Times New Roman belongs to the family of typefaces known as "serif". This describes the small extensions which sprout from the main strokes of letters in this font — such as those at the bottom of a capital T (T when formatted as Times) and at the end of the T's cross-bar. Futura, on the other hand, lacks these finesses and is known as a "sans serif" font.

A third category of fonts are the "decoratives".

These can be ornate typefaces used for eye-catching headings (but almost never for the main body of your work) or collections of symbols, icons and other glyphs often known as "dingbats". Symbol and Wingdings are decorative fonts supplied with Windows.

Most wordprocessing, desktop publishing and graphics programs come with dozens of TrueType fonts to add to your collection. If these aren't enough to sate your appetite, you can buy hundreds crammed onto a single CD for as little as £10.

QUICK TIP

It's nice to have hundreds of fonts at your fingertips, but you should never use more than two or three per page, lest your documents end up looking like a ransom note.

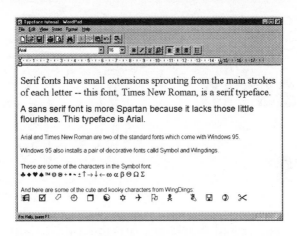

Windows stores all active typefaces in a special Fonts folder. You'll find a shortcut to this folder inside the Control Panel.

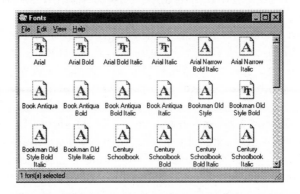

How many fonts can you have at your fingertips in Windows 95?

I've had 500 loaded without a drop in performance — a welcome change from Windows 3.1, which couldn't take more than a few dozen fonts without slowing down.

This said, it's folly to install more typefaces than you need, because you'll be forever scrolling through drop-down font lists in programs like Microsoft *Word for Windows*. It's best to settle on a selection of typefaces which you regularly use and stockpile the rest somewhere on your hard drive or a floppy disk. Just load them into the Fonts folder as needed.

Windows 95 includes a Font Viewer which lets you see what each font looks like, even if it's not installed: simply double-click on the font icon (in your Fonts folder which you will find in the Control Panel).

You can also print a sample page of this font to build a catalogue of all your fonts for later reference.

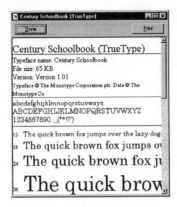

Adding and removing fonts

There are two ways to add fonts to your Windows 95 system.

1. Open the Fonts folder (click on the shortcut in Control Panel) and under the File menu select Install New Font.

Specify where Windows 95 will find the new font files (for example, on a CD-ROM in your drive), select the fonts you want to add, and finally check the box marked "Copy fonts to Font folder" and click OK.

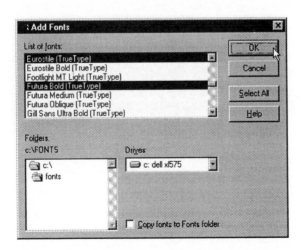

2. The easy way to add fonts is to Drag-and-Drop them. Select the font using Windows Explorer or from an open folder, then drag it across the screen and drop it into the open Fonts folder.

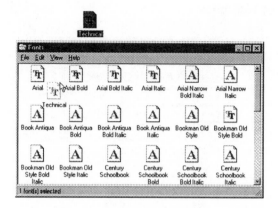

If you want to remove any typeface, you can do this by dragging it out of the Fonts folder into the Recycle Bin, or by choosing the Delete option under the folder's File menu.

A final note of caution: if you're using a sans-serif font such as Futura in your document and want to use another typeface as well, stick to sans-serif instead of using a serif face such as Times.

QUICK TIP

You can keep your fonts elsewhere on the hard drive and right-drag a shortcut of them into the Fonts folder — but if you delete the shortcut the original font file is also removed.

CHAPTER 11

Doing Windows Your Way

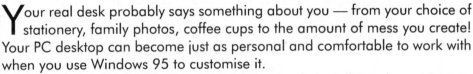

Your real desk probably says something about you — from your choice of stationery, family photos, coffee cups to the amount of mess you create! Your PC desktop can become just as personal and comfortable to work with when you use Windows 95 to customise it.

Let's begin with the look of your desktop and overall Windows 95 interface.

Right-click on the desktop and select Properties (or open the Control Panel and double-click on the Display icon). This is where all the action is.

Hang some wallpaper

By clicking on the Background tab you can choose a backdrop pattern and specify an image to be used as wallpaper.

If you choose to Tile the image you won't be able to see the Pattern, whereas centering the image will show the Pattern as a border.

Wallpaper images are simply computer picture files in "bitmap" (BMP) format. You can download new images from the Internet or even scan your favourite photo as a BMP image to use as wallpaper!

Save that screen!

Screen savers were created to prolong the life of old monochrome (single colour) monitors. An image constantly displayed on screen would "burn" itself into the picture tube, so that even when another image was shown a ghost-like residual of the former screen remained. You can see this effect on the screens of many automatic teller machines.

A screen saver prevented this by calling up a moving image when the machine hadn't been used for a certain period of time.

Although modern monitors aren't affected by burn, the market for screen savers remains. They've simply became a means of entertainment which puts the "personal" back into personal computing.

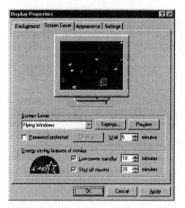

Make your choice from the screen savers supplied under the Screen Saver tab (also in the Display Properties dialog box), then click on the Settings button to customise your display.

To prevent other people using your PC while you're away, set a password by checking the "Password Protected" box and clicking on the Change button, then choosing your password. You can also adjust the energy-saving features of your PC monitor in this dialog box.

Your nearest computer store sells many screen saver programs which work with Windows 95 — the coolest belonging to Berkeley Systems' *AfterDark* line-up.

Colour your world

Select the Appearance tab (once again in Display Properties) to choose a preset Windows 95 colour scheme.

Or, if you're feeling creative, play Picasso and design your own colour scheme. Simply click on any part of the demonstration screen or choose an option from the drop-down Item list and then specify any colour or font — just don't forget to save your new scheme with a unique name.

Bigger Windows for a better view

Now let's look at the options under the Settings tab.

If you have a 15-inch monitor, increase your desktop area to 800 x 600 by dragging the slider one position to the right — the sample screen will show how your new desktop will look.

On most monitors you also have the opportunity to change the number of colours between 16, 256, High Colour and True Colour for added depth and pizzazz. The catch is that your computer has to work harder to produce these dazzling desktop displays, diverting memory and processing power away from your programs.

As a result of this your system will be slower and images on your screen will take longer to appear — although everything from desktop icons to photographic images are drop-dead gorgeous in High Colour.

I suggest you try each setting for a few days and decide which offers the right balance between glitz and grunt.

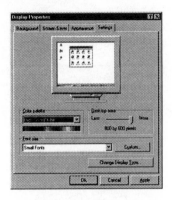

The Plus factor

Some PCs include an additional Microsoft program known as *Plus* (which you can also buy at most computer stores).

This add-on allows you to further customise Windows 95. One of the most attractive elements offered by *Plus* is desktop themes, which customises the Windows desktop with integrated collections of wallpaper, screen savers, icons, mouse cursors and even sounds.

Under the *Nature* theme, for example, the My Computer icon is transformed into a butterfly and the Recycle Bin becomes a small campfire. Cursors are shown as animations of sprouting flowers and crawling bugs, while events such as opening and closing Windows and making menu selections sound forth with the croaks of frogs and the buzz of cicadas. Even system fonts and colours take on a suitably earthy identity.

Other themes include *Leonardo da Vinci* (with sounds of Renaissance instruments), *Mystery* (your desktop is a dimly-light Victorian study echoing with the sounds of approaching footsteps, creaking doors and heartbeats), the tie-dyed splendour of the *1960s*, as well as *Travel, Nature, Science* and *Sports*.

To set these themes open the desktop Themes icon in the Control Panel. For more *Plus* enhancements look under the *Plus* tab in Display Properties.

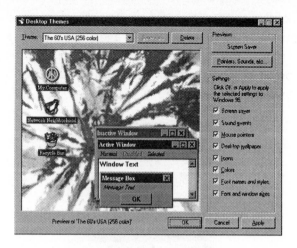

Horses for cursors

Tired of seeing that same old mouse pointer day in and day out?

Using the Mouse applet in Control Panel you can alter the cursors used by Windows. You'll find running horses, playing pianos, bananas peeling, coffee cups spilling and more. If you're still looking for inspiration, try the Internet.

Back Home

Many computer stores sell Windows 95 PCs without changing the system settings to reflect British standards in time, date and measurement.

Open the Control Panel, run the Regional Settings control and ensure the Regional Settings tab shows "English (British)".

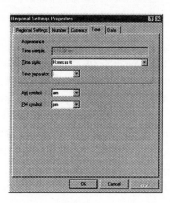

You may also want to change the digital clock in the Tray from military "2400" time to a more friendly format. To do this, simply click on the Time tab, and in the Time Style box enter (using lower case)

h:mm:ss tt

In the AM and PM Symbol fields enter "AM" (or "am" if you prefer).

The clock will now show "5:05 pm" instead of the more cryptic "17:05".

Sounds unlimited

Windows can be set to play sounds each time you start a program, empty the Recycle Bin or perform several other actions.

To inspect and change the current settings open the Control Panel and double-click on the Sounds icon.

The Windows 95 CD-ROM includes several sample sound schemes. If you get bored with these, check out the Internet for a wealth of additional sound clips.

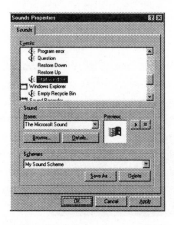

Use shortcuts

Shortcuts are one of the handiest inclusions in Windows 95.

For instance, wouldn't life would be a little easier if you had instant access to your drives without having to open My Computer every time? You can do this using shortcuts — simply open My Computer and drag the icons for your hard drive, floppy drive and CD-ROM drive onto the desktop.

Windows will respond by advising that you cannot move the item, but may create a shortcut to it instead. As this is what you were intending to do anyhow, click on "Yes" to create the shortcut. From now on, to copy a file to a floppy disk, you can simply drag the file icon onto the shortcut for your floppy drive.

To change the default shortcut name, right-click on the shortcut and choose Rename from the pop-up menu. The curly arrow in the lower-left corner of the icon will remind you this is a shortcut and not the original object.

You may also like to create shortcuts to the folders which you use most often, and to files which you launch several times each day. Simply select the folder or file on your hard drive or in Explorer, right-click on it and drag the icon onto the desktop. From the pop-up menu choose "Create Shortcut(s) Here" and Windows 95 will do the rest.

3½ Floppy (A)   Hard disk (C)   CD-ROM (D)   My Documents

It's just as easy to create a desktop shortcut to a program, such as your wordprocessor or personal organiser, and these can prove handy.

However, some of the beauty of Windows 95 lies in the uncluttered screen and deskspace — so beware of cluttering up your screen. I tend to keep my desktop fairly clean, with drive icons down one side and shortcut folders down the other.

Streamlining Start

The Start menu is the "home base" of Windows 95, so it's important that it feels comfortable and contains neither more nor less than you need.

QUICK TIP

If you're certain you want to delete a file (and are equally sure that you won't need to recover it) hold down the Shift key when you drag it to the Recycle Bin. This will delete it for good.

Begin streamlining Start by deciding whether you want large icons and the Windows 95 strip down the side of the pop-up Start menu. If not, right-click on an empty area of the Taskbar, select Properties from the pop-up menu and check the box marked "Show small icons in Start menu".

Programs which you use often can be placed at the top of your Start menu, rather than crowding your desktop with shortcuts. Simply drag any icon onto the Start button and watch as it sprouts a shortcut arrow, then release your mouse button and drop it. This creates a shortcut which appears above the Programs folder.

Did you know that the Start menu is actually a folder which lives in your Windows 95 directory?

To see it, right-click on Start and select Explore.

In the right-hand side of the Explorer window you'll see the contents of the Start folder — the Programs folder and any shortcuts you've dragged on to the menu.

In the left-hand column of the window the Start menu is shown as an open folder icon, containing the folder Programs.

To see the contents of the Programs folder click on the small "+" sign to the left of it — this display its sub-folders. It's this nesting of folders which you see every time you open the Start menu.

The Programs folder fills up very quickly — most applications add their own nested folders to it, while some (such as *Microsoft Office*) load their icons directly into it. A little organisation may come in useful — so create your own folders and shift those shortcut icons around until they appear exactly the way you want them.

Another organisational tip is to group some key applications in the Programs folder and place others in folders for specific tasks — such as the Internet — or group together all the programs you use for a regular project (such as creating a monthly newsletter).

To add a new folder to the Start menu, simply right-click on an empty area of the right-hand Explorer window, and select New Folder from the pop-up menu.

Shortcuts are small in size so you can have several shortcuts to the same program located in any folder where they are needed. If you use Microsoft *Publisher* to create a regular newsletter you could have one shortcut in a Microsoft folder and another in a Newsletter folder.

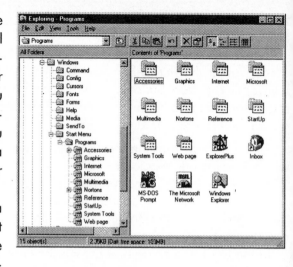

You can even place a folder at the top of the Start menu itself, just to avoid the extra step of opening the Programs folder. Maybe you spend a lot of time on the Internet: so why not create an Internet folder containing shortcuts to your Web browser, email software and newsreader, and have it sitting within easy reach atop the Start Menu?

In Windows Explorer select the Start Menu folder and right-click on an empty part of the right-hand Explorer window (in the same space as the Programs folder).

Select New Folder from the pop-up menu, name it Internet, then copy the relevant shortcut icons from other folders inside the Programs group.

Note that you can remove any unwanted items from the Start menu's folders — simply select the shortcut icon and drag it to the Recycle bin.

Don't be afraid to try any Start menu layout that takes your fancy. You can always change it back again — there are very few steps that will cause irreparable damage, and you'll receive plenty of warnings along the way to these.

In the end, customising your desktop will save you time and effort, and make working with Windows 95 easier and more intuitive.

Start me up

Place a shortcut to those programs and utilities which you rely on every day inside your Start Up folder, which you'll find inside the Programs folder on your Start menu.

Programs in the Start Up folder are automatically run every time you switch on your PC, saving you the time and hassle of doing it yourself. An specially good way to protect your PC from viruses and hard drive problems is to use the Start Up folder to load programs such as Norton Anti-Virus and Norton Utilities.

My own Start Up group includes over a dozen programs, such as a wordprocessor, personal organiser software, email, an anti-virus sentry and several neat shareware add-ons.

It takes an extra two minutes for the PC to load them all, so as soon as I hit the ON switch I wander downstairs and make my morning coffee. When I come back my PC is ready for work — and so am I!

To add a shortcut to the Start Up folder right-click on the Start button and from the pop-up menu choose Explore. This opens the Windows Explorer on the Start Menu folder. Click the + symbol next to the Programs folder and among the folders you'll see one labelled StartUp. This is what appears on the Start Menu as the Start Up group, and the shortcut icons inside StartUp represent the programs which run when you begin your Windows 95 session.

Browse through the Programs folder and other folders inside this, looking for those icons for the programs you'd like to load with Windows — maybe it's the calculator inside the Accessories folder.

Right-click the Calculator shortcut, then drag it onto the StartUp folder and release the right mouse button. From the pop-up menu choose Create shortcut(s) Here.

Moving the Taskbar

There's no hard-and-fast rule that says you *have* to leave the Taskbar where it is. You can reposition it at the top or on either side of the screen — simply by clicking on any vacant area of the Taskbar with the left mouse button and then dragging.

Ah, but you want to use every square inch of screen space?

Right-click on the Taskbar, choose Properties and click on Auto-Hide. The Taskbar will now lie low, until your mouse cursor hovers over its position on screen for a fraction of a second — at which time the Taskbar slides up to do your bidding. Move the mouse away and the Taskbar vanishes again.

Bin there, done that!

You may also want to have your say in how the Windows Recycle Bin works.

Files dropped into the Recycle Bin aren't actually removed from your hard drive until you choose to "empty" the bin, so Windows needs somewhere to stow them in the meantime. It does this by fencing off part of your hard disk, erecting a "Keep Out" sign to all other software and admitting only those files which you've chosen to delete.

By default the Recycle Bin lays claim to 10 per cent of your hard disk space. As most new PCs come with a 1.2Gb drive this allots the Recycle Bin an overly generous 120Mb — precious space which you can rather use for installing programs.

To decrease this value to a more realistic setting, right-click on Recycle Bin, choose Properties and click on the Global tab. See the slider marked "Maximum size of Recycle Bin (percent of each drive)"? Click the slide control with your mouse and drag it to the left to shrink the size of the Recycle Bin and increase the amount of available hard disk space.

I've got this wound down to 1 per cent, which still provides an ample 12Mb safety net on my 1.2Gb hard disk. If you have more than one hard drive, specify the ratio for each disk by selecting "Configure drives independently".

Windows also insists on questioning your life-or-death decision when you delete a file — that annoying "Are you sure you want to send such-and-such a file to the Recycle Bin?". At the foot of the same Global tab click and remove the checkmark next to the line "Display delete confirmation dialog" to turn-off this warning.

POWER TIP: A HARD DRIVE SHORTCUT

A shortcut to your hard drive will save you a surprising amount of time each day.

To create this shortcut, right-click on the hard drive icon (which you'll find in My Computer) and drag it onto the desktop.

Now, release the button and a pop-up menu will appear. Select Create Shortcut(s) Here.

A shortcut icon to your hard drive will appear on the desktop.

Rename the shortcut (this doesn't affect the original drive) if you wish.

Alternatively, create a shortcut by Dragging-and-Dropping the icon using the left mouse button.

Windows 95 will ask if you want to create a shortcut — click on "Yes", and follow the instructions above to rename it, if you wish.

TEN MINUTE TUTOR

Keeping Your Windows Clean

In some respects, your PC should be treated like your car. Just as you periodically check your car's tyre pressure, change the oil filter and give it a polish, it's wise to keep those Windows squeaky clean with regular care and maintenance.

Defragment your hard disk

While you may consider every document and application file to be a single entity, Windows 95 sees things a little differently.

Windows breaks each file into small chunks and places these on to hard disk areas called sectors. Ideally, chunks of the same file are slotted into adjacent sectors, so that Windows can read them consecutively.

At least, that's the way thing start out when Windows 95 is first installed.

However, as new files are added and old ones deleted, your hard disk becomes a chequerboard of sectors which are empty, full or somewhere in between. When Windows now loads a file, it writes each chunk into the first available space — even if these spaces are scattered all over the drive.

Files written in this way are called "fragmented files", and while fragmentation doesn't harm the file in any way, it does slow your system down. Loading fragmented files takes longer than usual, because Windows has to jump around the disk, assembling the file from different sectors.

The Disk Defragmenter included with Windows rearranges files on the hard drive so your data is better organised and file access speeds up.

To defragment a drive, click on the Start button and choose Programs, then Accessories, System Tools, and finally Disk Defragmenter.

Select the drive you wish to defragment (usually C:). It is possible to defragment a floppy disk, but the gain in access speed is so slight that it's barely worth the effort.

The Disk Defragmenter checks the disk, informs you of the fragmentation level, and recommends whether defragmenting is necessary. However, before beginning to defragment, it's a good idea to take a look at the Advanced options.

For best results select the "Full Defragmentation" and "Check for Drive Errors" boxes. Click on OK, then back at the Disk Defragmenter dialog box click on Start.

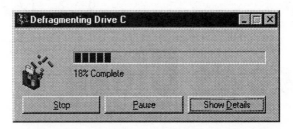

If you want to take a look at what's happening behind the scenes, click on the Show Details button. The Legend button will help you to make sense of it all.

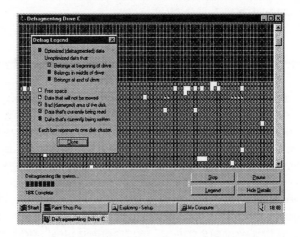

How often should you defrag? If you use your PC every day it's sensible to defrag on a weekly basis; otherwise, monthly will suffice. Remember to close all other programs before you use the Disk Defragmenter.

A healthy drive is a happy drive

All parts of your PC naturally suffer some degree of wear and tear.

Your hard drive, spinning away busily every minute of your computing day, is the most susceptible component. It's also the most crucial — if your hard drive fails, your data goes with it.

The Windows 95 ScanDisk utility keeps an eye on your hard drive, by giving it a quick physical check-up. If any section of the disk shows signs of wear and tear ScanDisk will either repair it or mark it off limits to data (so your work will not be stored on that area). ScanDisk also fixes "cross-linked" files which are often created when your system crashes and can contribute to software and system failures further down the track.

ScanDisk is located in the System Tools folder (found via Programs, then Accessories).

Select the drive to be checked, then choose either a Standard or Thorough test. Remember to check the "Automatically Fix Errors" box, otherwise you'll be prompted to respond to each error.

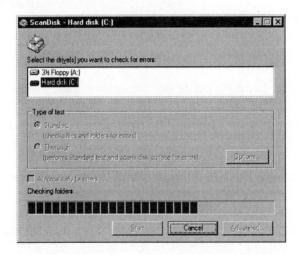

In the Advanced dialog box set "Lost File Fragments" to Free, "Cross-linked files" to "Delete" and click on the "Invalid file names" box in the "Check files for" option.

How often should you run ScanDisk? To be on the safe side I suggest once per week in Standard mode, once per month in Thorough.

Why backing up is hard to do

The process known as "backing up" — copying vital documents and files from your PC onto a removable medium such as floppy disk or special computer tape — is nothing less than essential PC housekeeping.

If your hard drive ever *does* crash and you've made a backup, you'll still have your most valuable files safe at hand. If not, you will have lost all your work: a major inconvenience for the average home PC user, and a nightmare for the modern business.

Windows 95 includes a Backup application, although it's often not installed on new PCs. Look inside the Start Menu's Programs-Accessories-System Tools folder. If there's no icon marked Backup you'll have to add it through the Control Panel's Add-Remove Programs applet, which you'll find in Control Panel.

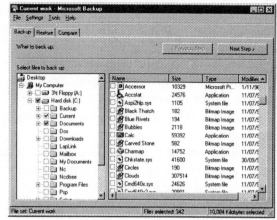

Backup makes it easy to safeguard your important files and folders — with the proviso that you have a backup tape drive, which is perhaps the least popular PC add-on of all time!

Backing up to floppy disks is not recommended. Floppy disks are too small and slow to be effective for modern backups — and the files created on the disks can only be used by Windows 95's Backup-Restore command (so you can't swap your documents across to a Windows 3.x machine).

Don't bother with Backup. Instead, head down to your nearest computer store and buy an Iomega Zip drive.

These neat-looking portable drives can store a whopping 100Mb of data on a single floppy-sized cartridge. They are fast, easy to install, simple to use, and good value at around £125 for the drive and £10 for each disk.

POWER TIP: CUTTING FILES DOWN TO SIZE

Windows 95 Backup is useful to transfer any file too large to fit onto a single floppy. For instance, the smallest version of Microsoft's Internet Explorer 3.0 weighs in at around 5Mb — over three times the size of a 1.4Mb diskette. You can run Backup and choose only this file, which Backup will split over four floppy disks. These disks can be sent to friends who can use Backup to "restore" and re-assemble the file on their Windows 95 PCs.

My own backup procedure is to use Windows Explorer to copy my Documents directory (containing all of my work in nested sub-folders) and other essential files onto a single 100Mb disk. I use additional Zip disks to store shareware and graphics and for archiving old material.

If you can't afford a Zip drive, just drag and drop your individual documents onto floppy disks — if necessary use a shareware archive utility like WinZip to reduce them to a fraction of their original size. You'll find a copy of WinZip in the shareware offer at the back of this book, or at WinZip's Internet home page at www.winzip.com.

How often should you back up your work?

I back up from my desktop computer to the Zip drive once a week. When travelling with my notebook PC I save each day's work onto a floppy disk every evening — just to be on the safe side.

DriveSpace: double or nothing?

If your hard disk is starting to feel crowded, consider using DriveSpace.

DriveSpace is a disk compression program that reduces the space used by the contents of your hard drive by up to half. The result is a hard disk effectively doubled in size.

The version of DriveSpace included in Windows 95 is disappointingly second-rate — it can't fully compress large hard drives, nor any drive containing more than 500Mb of data.

The Microsoft *Plus Pack* for Windows 95 contains the superior *DriveSpace* *4.0* which circumvents these problems — but opinion is divided on whether it is completely safe.

Ask around and you'll hear plenty of opinions on the joys and jeopardies of disk compression.

Personally, I avoid it.

Hard disk space is relatively cheap — my time and work isn't. I'd rather invest in a larger drive than trust my precious files to DriveSpace's voodoo.

Avoiding viruses

Viruses are annoying programs written by annoying people.

At best they're harmless but bothersome bits of code which cause your computer to display a message; at worst they can totally erase your data.

Software that is downloaded from the Internet or shared between friends is the main cause of virus infection. Documents created with the two most popular Windows applications, *Word* and *Excel*, can even hide embedded viral code which spreads throughout your system the minute you open the file.

All of this may cause your hand to tremble every time you power up your PC. Never fear — there are some precautions you can take:

❑ Don't share floppy disks

❑ Avoid suspect and pirate software and

❑ Invest in a good anti-virus program.

Always keep your anti-virus utility running in the background to detect sudden viral activity and act as a sentry against infected floppy disks, conduct scans of system files at start-up and check all files on a weekly basis.

Ensure your anti-virus utility program is kept up to date with the latest viral "definitions" so it can recognise new viruses.

Because Windows 95 has no inbuilt protection against viruses, the first piece of software you should buy is an anti-virus program.

Worthwhile programs to consider include *Dr. Solomon's Anti-Virus Toolkit*, the ever-popular and effective *McAfee Scan*, Symantec's *Norton Anti-Virus*, the interestingly named *PC-cillin*, *ThunderByte* and *VET*. All of these programs offer regular updates.

Solving system slow-downs

You may notice that your PC is slowing down — everything takes a bit longer, the hard drive spins more often and a few errors are starting to appear now and then.

The causes of system slow-down can be many and varied. However, a few simple tricks may just prove to be the cure.

❑ Defragment your hard drive. Many a fleet-footed hare becomes a creeping tortoise if the hard drive is 50 per cent fragmented.

❑ Keep your remaining hard disk space above 200Mb — empty the Recycle Bin, reduce the amount of space it reserves for deleted files and remove unnecessary programs if necessary.

❑ If your PC is anything less than a Pentium with 12Mb of RAM, avoid memory-gobbling frills such as Microsoft *Plus*, animated cursors and flashy wallpaper.

❑ Open the Control Panel, choose the System icon and click on the Performance tab. It should read "Your system is configured for optimal · performance". If not, use the online help system to track down and remedy any problems which are identified on the Performance sheet.

❑ Still no joy? Call a computer technician or roll up your sleeves and turn to chapter 14 for some self-help remedies.

POWER TIP: TAKING CONTROL

Getting to the Control Panel through My Computer or Settings (on the Start menu) can be cumbersome. There are, however, two winning ways to take control of your computer:

1. Create shortcuts. Open the Control Panel and right-drag frequently-used programs onto the desktop or the Start button to create a shortcut to them. This option works best when there are only a few control icons you use time and time again.

2. Move the Control Panel folder onto your Start menu. For lightening-fast access to the Control Panel, this tip is unbeatable, as it places a cascading Control Panel folder onto your Start menu!

To do this, right-click on the Start button and, from the pop-up menu, choose Explore. Now, right-click on a vacant area in the right-hand window pane of Explorer and click on New, Folder. Give this folder the following name — exactly as written, including the full stop and the curly brackets (note that there's no space between the full stop and the first curly bracket):

Control Panel.{21EC2020-3AEA-1069-A2DD-08002B30309D}

and hit Enter on your keyboard. Now, hit the Start button and you'll see Control Panel on the menu.

CHAPTER 12

Learning More About Windows 95

By this stage you should be well and truly up to speed with Windows 95. You've mastered the basics and beyond — indeed, don't be surprised if people start asking *you* for advice on all things Window-ish!

So where can you turn if you strike a spot of bother with Windows 95? What can you do to hone your skills and learn more about software and hardware?

Help is at hand

When you need answers, the first place to look is the Help files.

In all Windows programs these are accessed using the F1 key, or by choosing an option from the pull-down Help menu. In Windows 95 you can also reach Help via the desktop by clicking on Start and selecting Help.

The main Help screen in Windows 95 has three tabs.

Under the Contents tab the main areas of difficulty are grouped into "books". Click once on a book to open

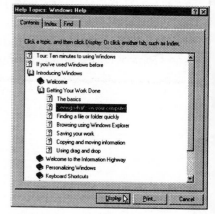

it, then select any page bearing a question mark and click on Display for help on that subject.

Many of the Windows 95 help screens contain step-by-step procedures and useful tips, as well as arrows to take you directly to the screen or folder you require.

Help's Index option can save you time — simply type the first few characters of the topic you need help with. A list of related topics will appear — highlight the one you want, then click on Display.

If you wish to search the entire Help file, click on the Find tab. Windows 95 will build a cross-referenced database of every word into the Help system, making it even easier to find what you want.

Specialised forms of help such as *Wizards,* which in some other software programs take the form of *Cue Cards* and *Coaches,* can also be used to lead you step by step through the more complex procedures.

Read all about it!

Keep up to date by reading the weekly computer sections of major newspapers, and monthly magazines such as *PC User* and *Your Computer.*

These publications have a strong focus on news, including reviews of recently released software.

The better magazines feature "buyer's guide" comparisons of software and hardware, as well as brief tutorials.

A good computer book can take you from zero to hero with Windows or any other software — but with many thousands of titles on the shelves, finding the right book is a challenge. Book reviews in computer magazines and first-hand reports from fellow computer users can help you to decide.

CHAPTER 13

Windows Ware

Julie Andrews counted several oddities among her favourite things — brown paper packages tied up with string, for starters. I hope my list of favourite freeware and shareware for Windows 95 is slightly more useful. (You can obtain copies of these programs from the shareware offer at the back of this book.)

I've deliberately kept this list fairly lean to cater for individual tastes. These programs are those which almost every Windows 95 user will enjoy — and there's plenty more where they came from!

If you want more, the Internet is your best source of up-to-date software. I recommend www.windows95.com as your first port of call.

PowerToys is a great collection of free Windows 95 add-ins written by some of the Windows 95 programmers, although it's not officially supported by Microsoft. It includes *TweakUI*, a handy Control Panel applet which fine-tunes many aspects of the Windows 95 desktop.

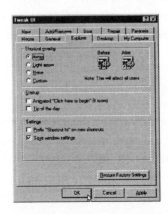

To magically squeeze programs and documents to a fraction of their original size archiving utilities such as *WinZip* are necessary. There's bountiful online help, a tutorial plus a Zip Wizard to assist beginners.

Many programs on the Internet are zipped and zipping email attachments will save you time and money.

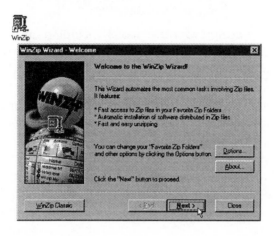

WinGO adds an icon to the system tray which, when clicked, shows a menu of shortcuts to a selected folder or directory — so you can quickly jump there. It's great for fast access to folders such as My Documents. You can even give each folder a plain language "alias", to make it easier to remember and find.

POWER TIP: DIALOG BOXES

Each dialog box in Windows 95 is, in essence, a miniature file manager.

Let's say you've used your wordprocessor to write a letter, but when you save the letter you decide that it really should be stored in a folder which doesn't yet exist. No problem — inside the File Save dialog box you'll find a small toolbar with a New Folder icon. Simply click on this to create the folder, then save the letter inside that file.

This same toolbar lets you sort files by name, type, size or date. You can also right-click any file to access several pop-up menu options, including Quick View, Delete and Rename.

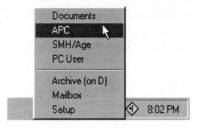

Would you like to design your own icons, including animation, to liven up your desktop? *MicroAngelo* has all the drawing tools you need. It can also extract icons from other programs, create icon libraries and change some of the standard icons used by the Windows 95 interface.

TrayIcon lets you use the System Tray as a program launcher, by loading icons representing applications into the Tray — a real time-saver compared to digging through the Start menu.

Then again, why not put the Start menu right at your fingertips?

That's what *SuperMenu* is all about. Click on the right mouse button anywhere on the desktop and the Start menu simply appears to do your bidding!

TrayExit lets you click on a door in the Taskbar Tray to shut down your PC or restart Windows.

StickIt creates sticky yellow notes which reside in the System Tray. You can have up to four different notes, each with their own page colour and alarms.

TopDesk provides access to all items on your desktop when they are buried several Windows deep.

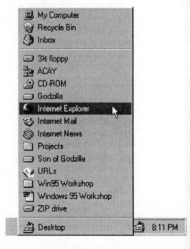

FinePrint saves you time and paper by squeezing two, four or eight printed pages onto a single sheet. It acts like a printer within Windows 95, with a dialog box to let you set the reduction size.

WinImage allows you to create disk "images" so you can quickly and easily make copies of disks from your hard drive. It also allows you to format a diskette in high capacity, including the special 1.7Mb DMF format.

WorldTimes adds a small earth icon to the System Tray, which displays the local time in up to four cities, relative to your own time zone.

TrayDay places an icon showing the current date in the System Tray.

WINDOWS ON THE WEB

There are dozens of places on the Internet dedicated to Windows 95. Try these:

Dylan Greene's Windows 95 Starting Page (www.dylan95.com) is one of the best for beginners. It contains a wealth of information, software and links to other Windows 95 pages.

On Frank Condron's World'o'Windows Page (www.conitech.com/windows) you'll find a great selection of the latest Windows news, tips and articles.

Mike Dixon's QAID Pages (www.kingsoft.com/qaid) is a "Question-Answer Information Database" containing tonnes of useful information, listed by topic and cross-referenced.

The Windows 95 & Mac Joke Wallpaper Page (www.jokewallpaper.com) is loaded with spoof wallpaper and screen savers poking fun at Microsoft and Windows. It's loads of laughs!

Windows 95 Annoyances (www.creativelement.com/win95ann) lists hundreds of less-than-amusing quirks of Windows 95 — and in most cases a clever way to get around them.

Microsoft's Windows 95 Home Page (www.microsoft.com/windows95) has Windows news, a "KnowledgeBase" of the most common software problems plus a library from where you can download add-ons and new components for Windows 95 .

Windows95.com (www.windows95.com) and The 32 Bit Software Archive (www.32bit.com) are the places to go for the latest freeware, shareware and trial versions of commercial programs.

Windows Sources (www.zdnet.com/wsources) and Windows Magazine (www.winmag.com) are the online versions of these two US Windows magazines.

You can also try any of the newsgroups beginning with the name "comp.os.ms-windows" to exchange messages with other Windows users around the globe.

CHAPTER 14

From Broken Windows to Safety Glass

In a perfect world your system would hum along day after day, week in and week out. Life just isn't like that, of course. Nor, for all Microsoft's efforts, is Windows 95.

It's as good an operating system as you can get for the modern home or small business PC. But things do go awry — with Windows 95, with various programs and with your hardware and peripherals.

Almost anyone who uses Windows on a daily basis has experienced some type of system error — ranging from low memory to a shuddering system crash. Often, the first you know about any type of error is after it has happened.

One of the more common errors is reported when a dialog box appears on screen advising that there is insufficient memory to complete a certain task. You can probably gain the upper hand by closing any other applications and trying again.

Windows 95 is fairly error-resilient, especially if you're running all 32-bit software. Unruly 16-bit and 32-bit applications can still cause a crash, but in many cases this will only close one application rather than shutting down the entire system.

I tend to reboot if my computer reports an error in a

QUICK TIP

You can run the Disk Defragmenter, Scan Disk and Backup directly from any drive inside My Computer. Simply right-click on the drive, choose Properties and click on the Tools tab.

significant component such as Explorer or a system file like USER or KERNEL, just to stay on the safe side.

Device drivers are a regular cause of conflict.

These small bits of software act as go-betweens with hardware (monitors, mouses, keyboards and all other plug-in devices) on one side and the operating system on the other

Many drivers are bundled with Windows — some designed for specific software, while others are generic (which means that they will work with most units).

Occasionally you'll need to load drivers supplied with the device, or update drivers for Windows 95. These issues can take some solving, but as a starting point ensure you are using the most up-to-date drivers.

Contact the supplier of your hardware or their tech support line — you can also download drivers directly from Internet if the manufacturer has a Web page.

Software conflicts can also be at the root of problems.

Two applications may stake a claim on the same chunk of memory, or an out-dated or corrupt file within the program itself may be to blame. In the latter case reinstalling the offending software is one solution.

POWER TIP: CREATING AND USING AN EMERGENCY DISK

Using a PC without an emergency startup disk is like driving without a seatbelt. Sure, nothing's going to happen. You're a safe and cautious driver who's never had an accident — but you should still belt up every time.

A startup or system disk is a seatbelt for your PC. Even if your computer has never given trouble, the very next time you turn it on could be the one time things go drastically wrong. And if you don't have an emergency disk, you'll wish you had! A startup disk contains the system files which will allow you to load Windows and save your documents onto a floppy disk, plus utilities to diagnose and repair basic problems.

Create a startup disk by opening Control Panel, running Add/Remove Programs and selecting the "Startup Disk" tab. Take a reliable 1.44Mb floppy, insert it into your floppy drive and click on Create Disk. You'll need to have your original Windows 95 CD-ROM or floppy disks at hand, to feed into the conputer as requested.

If one dark day Windows 95 refuses to load on your computer, insert the startup disk into your PC's floppy disk drive, turn off the PC and turn it on again.

Appendix

Installing Windows

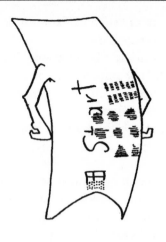

1. The first stage of the Windows 95 setup routine can be run from Windows 3.1 or MS-DOS.

In both instances Setup performs a routine check on your PC and, once it receives a clean bill of health, the Windows 95 *Setup Wizard* takes over and walks you through the rest of the procedure.

2. Install to the C:\WINDOWS directory only if the previous version of Windows has been removed (if this is applicable).

Conflicts between old and new pieces of software can slow your system and cause programs to halt or crash unexpectedly.

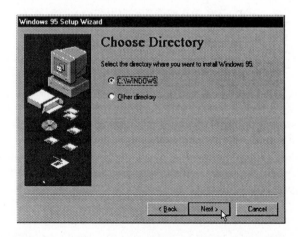

3. Four setup options will appear. These are fairly self-evident, but note that several key features are not included the *Typical* install — including the

Microsoft Network and Windows-based faxing, the Briefcase, Clipboard Viewer and Backup.

Similarly, if you are installing using a CD-ROM the online user's guide and tutorial are not included.

Custom is the best option to choose if you have room — despite the *Wizard's* claims, none of this is rocket-science stuff. All you'll have to do is check more boxes and click on a few buttons.

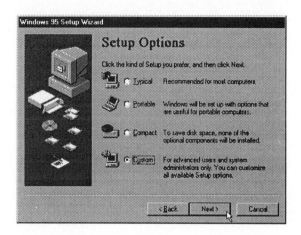

4. Windows 95 includes drivers for hundreds of common devices.

You can let the *Setup Wizard* do the walking, or specify your own mix of components. Either way, the *Wizard* will analyse your PC to see what's where. This process can take several minutes and cause a lot of rattling on your hard disk, so don't panic.

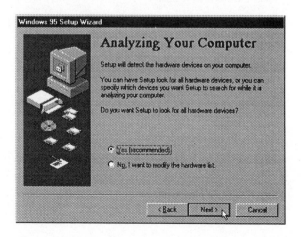

5. Many people think they have to choose *Microsoft Mail* to use electronic mail on the Internet.

Not so — Microsoft Mail is for Windows 95 computers connected to an office network, so only select this option if this is the case.

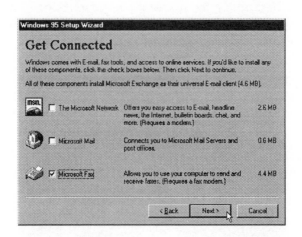

6. If you chose the Custom setup option you can now decide exactly what you want on your system.

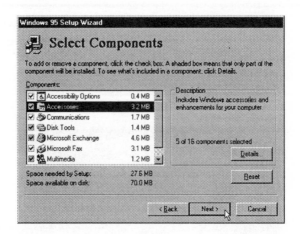

7. If you want to connect to the Internet you can remove the following components: Client for Microsoft Networks, Client for NetWare Networks, NetBEUI Protocol and IPX/SPX-compatible Protocol. Keep the Dial-Up Adaptor, which you'll need to call your ISP.

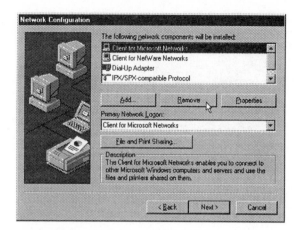

8. Now choose Add, select Protocol, and click Add again.

In the Select Network Protocol box choose Microsoft under Manufacturer and TCP/IP as the Network Protocol.

Click on OK and you're ready to surf in 32-bit style!

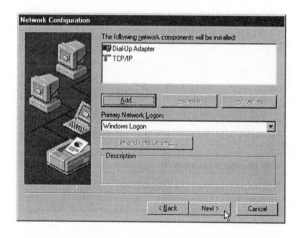

. Because you've chosen some network components Windows 95 thinks you'll be dialling into an office network. Humour it — this won't make any difference when you connect to your Internet Service Provider.

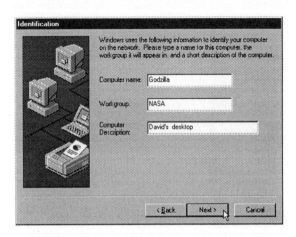

10. You can now check the results of Windows' automatic hardware detection.

If Windows has flagged an "Unknown Device", you will need to click on the Change button and choose the component yourself.

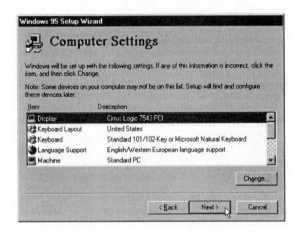

11. Yes, you *do* want a startup disk. Absolutely. If for some reason Windows 95 fails to reboot properly you could be stuck without any operating system on your PC.

Grab a spare disk (I prefer a brightly coloured one, so it stands out from the crowd), label it accordingly and continue the setup.

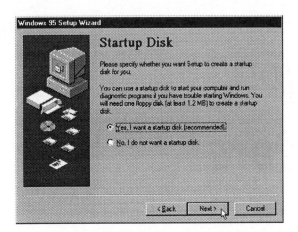

12. Breath easy — you're in the home stretch.

Windows will now copy itself onto your PC's hard disk and set up the Control Panel, Help system and Start menu groups. You'll also be prompted to set the correct system time and date, among other minor details. Then it's — next stop, Windows 95!

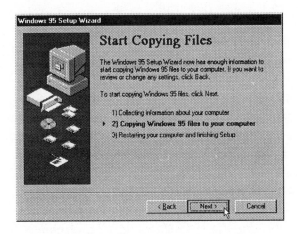

Glossary

Jargon Busters!

16-bit

Before the advent of Windows 95, operating systems, application software and utilities were written in computer code which could only process 16 bits (16 pieces of code) at a time, due to the less powerful computers of the day.

16-bit operating systems and 16-bit software are inherently slower than their 32-bit equivalents.

32-bit

The Windows 95 operating system and software are written for the latest computers, and can churn through 32 bits of code at a time.

While they are not automatically twice as fast as 16-bit software, there is a definite improvement in speed.

386

The model number of a computer CPU chip (produced by Intel) which was popular during the late 1980s and early 1990s. The 386-model chips were fast enough for MS-DOS and Windows 3.x, provided they had enough memory or RAM. Variations on the 386 were the 386SX and 386DX.

486

In the early to mid 1990s the 386 was superseded by a complete family of 486 chips, ranging from the 486DX to the progressively more muscular 486DX2 and 486DX4. These made light work of even the most demanding Windows 3.x software, such as desktop publishing and graphics.

586

The next generation of the 486 line. 586 chips are considered compatible to and competitive with Intel's Pentium chips.

Applet

A small piece of application software or utility program. Many of the accessories which come with Windows 95 are called applets.

Application

Many people use the terms application and utility interchangeably but, for the pedants (and I'm one!), there *is* a difference.

Application software mirrors a task in the real world environment and produces a document. Thus, word processing (which replaces the typewriter and produces letters, memos and so on) is an application — as is a database, desktop publishing, graphics and other similar programs.

CPU

Central Processing Unit. This small black computer chip is the engine of your personal computer. The 386, 486, 586 and Pentium chips are all CPUs.

Crash

Not an event to bring a smile to your face, a crash is the most serious of computer glitches. During a crash the PC screen freezes, refusing to respond to any keyboard action or mouse click, or a blue screen appears informing you that an error has occurred.

Sometimes Windows 95 can recover if you leave it alone for a minute or two. On other occasions Windows will restart your PC from scratch — or you'll have to do the same by turning it off, then on again.

Defragment

The process whereby files on your hard drive which are broken into small, non-sequential chunks are joined and ordered into complete files. This can improve the speed and performance of your computer.

Desktop

The screen which appears when you start Windows 95, and is visible when no programs are running or these have been minimised into the taskbar. The desktop holds the icons for My Computer and the Recycle Bin as well as any files, folders or shortcuts you choose to place there.

Dialog box

When Windows 95 needs information to be input, it displays a dialog box. Everyday examples include the Recycle Bin warning which queries "Do you really want to delete this file?", or the screen which appears when you choose File-Open inside your wordprocessor.

Double-click

The action of clicking the main (usually left) button on your mouse twice and in rapid succession — click-click! Use a double-click to run a program.

Drag and drop

The action of holding down a mouse button (usually the left button) over an icon or other object to select it and, without releasing the button, moving the mouse so the object is dragged across your screen to a particular location. When it reaches the desired location releasing the mouse button causes the object to be dropped there.

Folder

A place on your hard drive, floppy disk or desktop where you store documents and other files. In MS-DOS and Windows 3.1 folders are known as directories. The main difference between directories and folders is that Windows 95 folders can have long names.

Freeware

Software which is given away, usually over the Internet, without requiring the user to pay for it.

GUI

Pronounced "gooey", this is how computer nerds talk about the Graphic User Interface — how an operating system or other piece of software interacts with the user. It's graphical because it employs icons instead of long lines of text.

Icon

A small on-screen picture which represents an object and its function.

For example, the Recycle Bin employs the trash can icon to indicate that you use the Bin to dump or delete files. The icon for My Computer rather sensibly looks like a computer (unless you choose to change it) and so on.

Maximised

A program's window is maximised when it occupies the entire screen. This gives you the largest possible area to use for creating a graphic, working on a spreadsheet, or viewing a page, for example.

Minimised

A program's window is minimised when shrunk into the Taskbar at the bottom of the Windows 95 screen. You can only see the window as a thin button on the Taskbar.

It's useful to minimise a program when you plan to use it a little later but want it out of the way right now. Your other option is to close the program completely and, when you need it, launch it from the Start Menu.

Microsoft

The world's largest software company, founded by multi-billionaire Bill Gates.

Microsoft programmers wrote the MS-DOS, Windows 3.1 and Windows 95 operating systems, as well as best-selling software such as *Office*, *Word for Windows* and *Publisher*.

MS-DOS

When IBM was building their first personal computer they needed a "disk operating system" — an operating system which could handle all the files on a floppy disk, as there were no hard drives at the time. This DOS had to be compact and (for its time) easy to use. They chose a DOS from Microsoft (the company's name is where the "MS" comes from), loaded it onto all of their PCs and the rest, as they say, is history.

Multitasking

Your computer is capable of multitasking when it can undertake more than one task at a time — such as copying a file while you print a document and surf the Internet.

"Multi-threading" means that an individual program can do several things at once. A multithreaded wordprocessor, for example, allows you to print one document while you edit another, instead of freezing the screen until the printing has finished.

Online help

Rather than dive for a printed manual when you need assistance, use the online help files which are included in all modern software. These screens appear on your computer when you choose the Help menu or hit the F1 key.

Operating system

Special software which breathes life into your computer so you can tell it what to do. Sometimes abbreviated to OS, the operating system also lets you run applications, utilities and games.

MS-DOS and Windows 95 are two operating systems. Macintosh computers use the MacOS, while IBM now has their own system called OS/2.

Pentium

Intel's current king of the PC processors is the Pentium chip, with an even more souped-up version called the Pentium Pro. The Pro is already used in high-end graphics machines and is likely to overtake the standard Pentium sometime in 1998, although your current Pentium will be sufficient for a few years to come.

Plug and Play

The teamwork between Windows 95 and any piece of hardware, such as a printer or sound card, which lets Windows recognise and automatically configure the item without the user needing to load special software, fiddle with switches and so on.

RAM

Random Access Memory is where a computer stores the software while you are using it (when you close a program all the data is returned to your hard drive).

The more RAM you have, the more your computer can do. With Windows 95 you want at least 16Mb of RAM.

Right-click

The action of clicking the secondary mouse button, almost always the one on the right. In most of Windows 95 this calls a special pop-up menu of options.

Single click

Pressing the primary (left) mouse button and then releasing it. A single click is used to select an item on the Windows 95 desktop or in Explorer, access a pull-down menu, launch the Start Menu or activate a button on a toolbar.

Shareware

"Try before you buy" software, which you can evaluate in your own time, and only pay a registration fee to the authors if and when you decide to keep it. Registration often offers additional benefits, such as manuals and assistance.

Toolbar

A strip of icons or buttons which sit just below a program's menu.

These buttons represent the most often-used commands, and can provide time-saving shortcuts. For example, you can click a button to save a file without having to pull down the File menu and select the Save option.

Trialware

A sample version of software which you can use for a set period, usually 30 days, or on which some significant features have been limited or disabled. Trialware gives you a taste of the program before you need to splash out on the full version.

Utility

A breed of program devoted to tasks which specifically concern your computer, as opposed to programs designed to produce "work". Virus detectors, defragmenters, file transfer software and backup programs all belong to the category of utility software.

Virus

Nasty anti-social programs written by nasty anti-social people.

Viruses are spread on floppy disks, by downloading files from the Internet and even opening a wordprocessing document created on another computer. They can flash annoying messages or erase whole chunks of data.

Use an anti-virus utility to watch out for and eliminate these bugs. Note, however, that these programs need to be regularly updated to recognise and combat the latest and most deadly monsters.

Windows

The Windows family of operating systems developed by Microsoft: Windows 3.x, Windows 95, and more recently Windows NT and Windows CE.

Windows 3.x

A phrase used to describe the older 16-bit releases of Microsoft Windows: editions 3.0, 3.1 and 3.11.

Windows 95

The latest and greatest version of Windows, and the subject of this book.

Windows NT

An "industrial-strength" version of Windows designed for use by banks, large companies and multi-national corporations.

Windows CE

A "diet" version of Windows 95 designed to run on handheld computers and exchange data with a Windows 95 desktop or notebook PC.

Shareware and Freeware Offer

⇨ **Continued from page 4**

DISK WIN-5

Includes a stunning range of **clipart images** ready to import into your DOS and Windows applications.

DISK WIN-6

Personal Information Manager - The easiest PIM you will ever use. A full drag and drop interface is included with a perpetual calendar and planner to the year 9000. CallerID support, Logging of calls, Birthday/Anniversary support! 3-D, professional look. Rolodex Style Phonebook w/ Yellow and White Pages, customisable fields and fast searches. Fax using Delrina's WinFax Pro. Create letters, schedule appointments, dial phone, mail merge. Edit and save text, create reports of phonebook. Make envelopes, import/export data and much more.

DISK WIN-7

Includes: **List-It** - user friendly, menu driven Personal Property Inventory program that keeps your valuable property in alphabetical order and with the Quick View Feature as close as a click of the keyboard. Will print a dated report to place in your file in case of theft or fire. (Windows and DOS)

That's Music! will help you keep track of all of your CDs and tapes in a simple, easy to use, database. Store the title, artist(s), year, type of media, your personally defined category, and every song on each CD or tape with ample room for notes, writers, or anything else you require. Keep a separate database for each type of music you own.

Automotive Repair Database - 200+ options with colour pull-down menu and over 200 windows full of technical information. Very easy to use, has a number of built in utilities.

Auto Bypass - Allows you to easily choose to load or bypass loading programs as your PC starts up.

DISK WIN-8

Includes: **Windows Gourmet** - Powerful but easy recipe database and meal planning system. Familiar "recipe card" display and simple interface allows for quick entry and indexing of hundreds of recipes. Easily group a series of recipes together into a single meal and adjust servings to account for any yield. Prints shopping lists, as well as individual recipes. Can retrieve and save Meal Master text files.

Sports Card Catalogue - Input as much detail as you need, including the year of issue, brand, card number, team, type, description, date and price of purchase, and more. Unlimited number of entries, automatically sorted. Searching by any field, printing, graphs, and more. On-line help messages only one mouse click away.

Jigsaw Puzzle game - Full realistic display and operation. Object oriented for you to feel like playing a real game!. From 25 to more than 400 pieces. Boxes, nails, rankings, scores. Just pick anything with your mouse and enjoy. For puzzle enthusiasts of all ages.

DISK WIN-9

Dino Numbers - Exciting arithmetic game for 7-12. Help Derik the Dinosaur rescue cows from Rex the Tyrannosaurus by solving various math tasks (add, subtract, multiply, or divide). Includes animation, music, and sound effects. Req: 386+; Win 3.1, Win95, , or OS/2; 4MB RAM; Sound Card (optional, but recommended).

DISK WIN-10

Dino Spell - Spelling game for ages 7-12. Help Derik the Dinosaur rescue fruit from Rex the Tyrannosaurus by solving various spelling challenges. Includes animation, music, and sound effects. Req: 386+; Win 3.1, Win 95, or OS/2; 4MB RAM; Sound Card (opt).

Turn to page 128 for details of how to get your disks

The Complete Beginner's Guide to The Internet

Everywhere you turn, it's Internet this, Cyberspace that and Superhighway the other. Indeed, hardly a day goes by without us being bombarded with information and reasons why everyone should be on the Net. But none of that is of much help in making an informed decision about joining and using the Internet.

What exactly is The Internet? Where did it come from and where is it going? And, more importantly, how can everybody take their place in this new community?

The Complete Beginner's Guide to The Internet answers all of those questions and more. On top of being an indispensable guide to the basics of Cyberspace,

❏   It is the lowest priced introduction on the market by a long way at a surfer-friendly £4.95. Who wants to spend £30+ on an alternative to find out The Internet is not for them?

❏   It comes in an easy-to-read format. Alternatives, with their 300+ pages, are intimidating even to those who are familiar with The Net, let alone complete beginners!

❏   Each reader will be eligible for 10 hours FREE Internet access, FREE Internet software and a FREE month's membership to CompuServe (a total package worth over £15).

ISBN: 1-873668-14-7
Price: £4.95

The Complete Beginner's Guide to The Internet tells you:

● What types of resources are available for private, educational and business use,
● What software and hardware you need to access them,
● How to connect to and use The Internet via a modem or network,
● How you go about finding what you want,
● How to communicate with others, and
● The rules of the Superhighway, or 'netiquette'.

Features a greatly expanded section on The World Wide Web, step-by-step instructions on using a search engine, more detail on the benefits of and how to use email, plus new chapters on Internet Relay Chat and Multi-User Dungeons (Internet games).

About the Author

Mark Neely is Managing Director of AccessNT Ltd, a company that specialises in advising clients on Internet connectivity issues and offers in-house training and technical support. Mark has conducted numerous 'Introduction to the Internet' courses for educational and business users alike. He is also the author of The Experts Business Guide to The Internet and Parents, Teachers and Students Guide to The Internet.

Free Internet Access and software worth over £15

Order form for all books on page 126

The Complete Beginner's Guide to Making Money on The Internet

"I would highly recommend this book as both a learning tool for someone contemplating the Internet and for use by the more experienced user as a memory jogger. An excellent publication."
David Siggs, Managing Director, Business Opportunity World

In 1994, businesses clocked up more than £130 million in sales over the Internet. Within one year that figure had risen to £300 million and was still growing almost exponentially!

These on-the-net businesses used the Internet to slash costs; decrease the cost of customer support; reduce purchasing costs; cut marketing expenses and to reach hitherto untapped markets. Their secrets are revealed in this book, so that you can make money on the Internet before your competitors beat you to it.

You'll find answers to the following questions:
● Is the Internet right for my business?
● How can I use the Internet to get and keep customers?
● Can I get started quickly and cheaply?
● What are the potential problems?
● How can I avoid costly mistakes?

It does not matter what type of computer or software you have from IBM, Windows '95, Macintosh or OS/2, you can benefit from this book to make money on the Internet.

ISBN: 1-873668 18 X   *Price: £3.95*

Tax Self Assessment Made Easy

Like it or not, the biggest change to the UK tax system has taken place. Self assessment is already in place for many taxpayers who may not even know it. Can it be ignored? No! New requirements for keeping records for example, or changes in the date for submitting tax returns will affect NINE MILLION people according to The Revenue. Penalties for not keeping records can be £3,000, whilst late tax returns can be charged at up to £60 per day.

Thankfully, Stefan Bernstein has distilled all the jargon down to a simple easy to follow guide **at a price the ordinary taxpayer can afford.** The book tells you what you have to do and when to do it, warning you of what happens if you don't.

ISBN: 1-873668-09-0   **Price: £5.99**

Internet Guide for Teachers, Students & Parents

Many schools are only just beginning to realise the benefits of providing Internet access for both teachers and students. Others are undecided whether Internet access will be a benefit . . . or a burden. And there's always that nagging question - how much will it cost?

This guide looks at using the Internet in education, with down-to-earth advice on many issues, including how to:

- Design lessons involving the use of the Internet in the classroom.
- Plan and organise an Internet connection for any school.
- Publish a Student Newspaper on the World Wide Web.
- Make contact with other teachers and students around the world to share ideas, experiences and cultures.
- World Wide Web as a search tool.

ISBN: 1-873668-53-8

Price: £9.95

Mark Neely also highlights the hidden dangers lurking in cyberspace, offering sensible advice to teachers and parents on how to protect children from undesirable material on the Internet.

The Expert's Business Guide to The Internet
Also by Mark Neely

The Internet is changing and evolving literally every day, each change bringing with it new opportunities and ideas for promotion and marketing. And this guide helps you explore all aspects of establishing yourself in this huge marketplace.

Written specifically for businesses wishing to establish a strong Internet presence, it takes you through the issues surrounding the development of electronic commerce (the digital economy) by explaining in **non-technical terms** what business on the Internet is all about.

The author closely examines the social dynamics and popular culture of the Net, which will play a large part in any strategy to commercially harness Cyberspace.

FREE UPDATES

Register, free of charge, to gain exclusive access to weekly on-line updates. All the latest news, plus columns on technologies and market strategies as well as links to hundreds of other Internet marketing and business-related sources.

You could say this book won't go out of date!!

Price: £24.95 including free updates

Also, in everyday language:

- What tools are available to help you incorporate the Net in your normal activities.
- What constitutes acceptable commercial activity on the Net - and what could cause your company to be 'flamed'.
- How to develop an integrated Internet strategy.
- How to ensure your business procedures compliment - not contradict - your Net activities.
- Privacy and Security when dealing with digital cash.

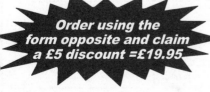

Order using the form opposite and claim a £5 discount =£19.95